Colorad'

D1683078

STAFF TRAINING
AND RECOGNITION
PROGRAM

Written by Catherine Izor
Produced by Jeremiah Cahill and Rena Crispin
Center for Professional Development
CUNA & Affiliates

Copyright © 1988, 1990, 1995, 2001
Credit Union National Association, Inc.

ISBN 0-7872-7511-5

All rights reserved. No part of this publication may
be reproduced, stored in a retrieval system, or
transmitted, in any form or by any means, electronic,
mechanical, photocopying, recording or otherwise,
without the prior written permission of the copyright
owner.

Printed in the United States of America

10 9 8 7 6 5 4 3 2 1

MEMBER
SERVICES

(S110)

(Fourth Edition)

 KENDALL/HUNT PUBLISHING COMPANY
4050 Westmark Drive P.O. Box 1840 Dubuque, Iowa 52004-1840

With respect to the content of this publication, neither the Credit Union National Association, Inc. (CUNA) nor any of its affiliates or its or their respective employees make any express or implied warranty or assume any legal liability or responsibility for the accuracy, completeness, or usefulness of any information, commercial product, service, process, provider, vendor, or trade name/mark that is disclosed. References to any specific commercial product, service, process, provider, vendor, or trade name/mark in this publication also do not necessarily constitute or imply that such product or provider is endorsed, recommended, or warranted by CUNA. The views and opinions of the authors expressed herein do not necessarily state or reflect those of CUNA and such reference shall not be used for advertising or product endorsement purposes.

This publication is designed to provide accurate and authoritative information in regard to the subject matter covered. It is sold with the understanding that the publisher, Credit Union National Association, Inc., is not engaged in rendering legal, accounting, or other professional services. If legal advice or other expert assistance is required, the services of a competent professional should be sought.

Contents

	Acknowledgments	iv
	About the Author	iv
	Preface	vi
	Introduction	**1**
Chapter 1	**Introduction to Credit Union Services**	**3**
Chapter 2	**Opening and Administering Membership Accounts**	**13**
Chapter 3	**Savings Accounts**	**35**
Chapter 4	**Share Draft Accounts**	**53**
Chapter 5	**Credit Union Lending**	**67**
Chapter 6	**Types of Loan Programs**	**81**
Chapter 7	**Transaction Systems**	**103**
Chapter 8	**Other Services**	**127**
Appendix A	**Answers to Activities**	**139**
Appendix B	**Glossary**	**141**
Appendix C	**Resources**	**149**
Appendix D	**Test Questions**	**157**
	Index	**165**

Acknowledgments

The author would like to thank the following organizations that provided assistance and documents for the latest edition of this module:

- Heartland Credit Union, Madison, Wisconsin
- Xerox Federal Credit Union, El Segundo, California
- Dane County Credit Union, Madison, Wisconsin
- Rogue Federal Credit Union, Medford, Oregon
- LANCO Federal Credit Union, Lancaster, Pennsylvania
- Visa USA

An earlier edition of *Member Services* was written by Denice Bruce, with contributions by Jeanne Engle and Bruce Shawkey.

About the Author

Catherine Izor has over twenty-five years' experience in the financial services field and has held management positions within financial institutions and a consulting company. She holds an M.A. in adult instructional management from Loyola University in Chicago and has presented programs on financial services topics to national and local audiences. Currently, she concentrates on authoring publications and computer-based training programs in the financial services field. For CUNA, she has written STAR modules on technology, career planning, share accounts, and lending.

The **Staff Training and Recognition (STAR)** program is designed to benefit all credit union staff members. The STAR program is divided into separate learning tracks. To be eligible for a STAR certificate and lapel pin, you must successfully complete all modules in the learning track you have chosen to pursue.

The Staff Training and Recognition (STAR) Program

Core Modules Required for All Tracks		
S010 Credit Union Orientation S020 Member Relations S030 Security		
Tracks	**Track Modules**	
Member Services	S100 S110 S120	Money and Negotiable Instruments Member Services Cross-Selling
Consumer Lending	S200 S210 S220	The Lending Process Lending Products and Regulations Collections
Credit Union Accounting	S300 S310 S320	Basic Accounting Accounting for Credit Unions Credit Union Financial Analysis
Advanced Lending	S400 S410 S420	Bankruptcy and Court Proceedings Mortgage Lending Loan Marketing
Credit Union Sales	S500 S510 S520	Improving and Maintaining Quality Service Successful Sales Techniques Interpersonal Skills: Understanding Your Impact on Members
Credit Union Technology	S600 S610 S620	Credit Union Technology Working with Technology Serving Members with Technology
Loan Officer	S700 S710 S720	Loan Interviewing Loan Underwriting Loan Servicing
Savings Plus	S800 S810 S820	Opening New Accounts Individual Retirement Accounts Investment Choices for Members
Credit Union Security	S900 S910	Preventing Fraud Security Issues
Professional and Career Development	S1000 S1010 S1020	Develop a Career Plan: Practical Tools and Methods for Mapping Your Career Write Effectively: Credit Union Business Writing Techniques Make Work Manageable: Time, Stress, and Workload Management Strategies
Member Services Level II	S1100 S1110 S1120	Working Effectively with Difficult Members and Staff Helping Members Understand and Solve Problems: Your Role as Financial Educator Using Technology to Improve Member Service

Preface

About These Modules

The STAR modules are not intended to provide legal advice, and we do not guarantee the information is appropriate for all state-chartered credit unions. If you have any legal or policy questions, contact your credit union president or your credit union league.

How to Use This Module

If you are sight-impaired and choose to have this module read to you, we suggest that a spouse, friend, or volunteer from your credit union or credit union league assist you. You can also check with your local library regarding reader services available in your community.

If you are participating in a seminar, your instructor will get you started.

If you are completing this module through correspondence study, please follow this procedure:
1. Read the chapter opening objectives to get an idea of what's ahead.
2. Read the module. Complete the activities as you read each chapter.
3. When you have read the module and completed the activities, take the competency test.

Competency Test Instructions

Each module in the STAR program has a competency test of forty multiple choice questions. To successfully complete the module, you must correctly answer at least thirty-two questions. You can refer to the module as you take the test, but the test must be completed individually.

If you are participating in a seminar, your instructor will provide directions. If you are completing this module through correspondence study, please follow this procedure:
1. Locate the test questions in the last appendix of the module.
2. Find a quiet place where you can work undisturbed and at your own pace.
3. Record your answers on the answer sheet that was mailed to you along with the module. Follow the instructions on this sheet for marking answers.
4. Complete the identification section on the answer sheet and make sure you have marked an answer for each question.
5. Mail the scannable answer sheets to CUNA's National Processing Center in the envelope provided. Mail competency test answer sheets to your league education department.

Introduction

Credit unions now offer a greater variety of services and a higher level of financial sophistication than at any other time in their history. To meet the needs of members, credit unions need better trained, more knowledgeable, and more professional employees. Members expect that credit union employees who assist them are informed and can provide accurate and up-to-date information about the financial services available at the credit union.

Studying this **Member Services** module can be tremendously helpful in your career. As the credit union movement continues to evolve, credit unions have found that technically competent employees with a solid understanding of available services are a valuable asset.

In this module, you will study a broad range of member services. Chapter 1 introduces you to credit union services and how they satisfy members' needs. You will also learn about credit union service organizations (CUSOs) that help credit unions by providing services beyond the ones allowed under credit union laws. Chapter 2 covers opening and administering membership accounts. You will learn about account ownerships and the requirements for opening new accounts. In addition, the chapter reviews key features of services offered to special member groups such as children and older members.

Chapter 3 explores the different types of credit union savings accounts. It covers how dividends are computed and characteristics of regular share savings accounts, share certificates, and money market accounts. It also presents information on types of retirement accounts.

In Chapter 4, you will study share draft accounts, possibly the most important service at credit unions. You will learn how share drafts travel through the check clearing system. You will also review the typical features and benefits of share draft accounts.

Chapter 5 lays down a foundation of knowledge about credit union loan concepts. It helps you understand open-end and closed-end credit, secured and unsecured credit, and how borrowers are evaluated for creditworthiness. You will also study how repayment risk and other factors affect loan rates.

Chapter 6 reviews the many types of credit union loan programs. You'll learn the features and benefits of signature (personal) loans, lines of credit

Member Services

INTRODUCTION

(including share draft overdraft protection), credit card accounts, education loans, business loans, vehicle loans and other options, first mortgage loans, home equity loans, home equity lines of credit, and other loans such as share account loans and stock loans.

Chapter 7 takes a different approach to services by looking at the various transaction systems, or methods members use to access their accounts and make transactions. You will explore automatic transfers, ATM/debit cards, telephone services, and Internet-based financial services. Internet services continue to expand every year and credit unions are taking advantage of the possibilities.

Chapter 8 concludes the module by considering a number of other services. Credit unions provide check services, safe deposit boxes, financial education, insurance, and financial planning and investment services. These services complete the wide array of services that credit unions offer members today.

Chapter 1 Introduction to Credit Union Services

Your credit union exists to provide financial services to its members. It's really that simple. However, the number and type of services vary from one credit union to another, depending on asset size, characteristics of the members, strategic mission, plus many other variables. For example, a small credit union that has a membership group of the employees of one local company may focus on a limited group of services where the credit union can give its members advantages over other local financial institutions. Or, a large credit union that serves employees of a company that has worldwide operations may put significant emphasis on electronic ways to deliver services rather than investing in a large branch network. The services your credit union offers reflect its characteristics and the needs of its members.

In this chapter, you will gain an understanding of why you need to learn about a broad range of credit union services. You will also understand the members' perspective on credit union services and how they satisfy members' financial needs.

Objectives

Upon completion of this chapter, you will be able to

1. **explain reasons to learn about a wide range of credit union services;**
2. **describe categories of members' financial needs that credit union services can satisfy;**
3. **list examples of typical credit union services;**
4. **match credit union services to members' financial needs;**
5. **define *credit union service organization (CUSO)* and explain how it supports credit union operations and provides financial services to members.**

Why Learn about Credit Union Services?

It is important for you to know basic information about the full range of services that your credit union provides. This knowledge helps you in the following ways:

- perform your own job more competently
- give professional referrals to other employees
- give high-quality member service
- make cross-sales effectively

- help your credit union compete successfully against other financial institutions
- prepare yourself for the future

Perform Your Own Job More Competently

Obviously, your first priority in product and service knowledge is to thoroughly know the services you personally support. If your job is lending, you need a substantial knowledge of loans. If your job is opening new accounts, you need a thorough knowledge of savings accounts, certificates, and share draft accounts. This knowledge helps you perform your job with little assistance and increases your professionalism.

For certain services you support, you may need to be an expert who knows all the details and unusual aspects. You may be one of a select few who knows all the "ins and outs" of a service. To gain this knowledge, your training, experience, and personal efforts to learn more will contribute to your success.

Give Professional Referrals to Other Employees

For services outside your area of responsibility, you need enough knowledge to help direct members to the right employees. To make good referrals, you need to know

- **What the service is, basic features, and your credit union's "name" for it.** For example, if your credit union has a children's club with a mascot, you need to know the name of the mascot. That way, if a child asks about "Chuckie the woodchuck" you'll know what he or she means.
- **Where a member can obtain a brochure on the service (if one is available).** Direct members to brochure racks or keep brochures at your workstation or desk. Always make sure you have the latest brochure. Simply reading the brochures yourself can teach you a lot about the service and what information you can quickly pass along to a member.
- **Who handles the service.** When a member wants to sign up for a service you don't handle, or simply has questions, you need to be able to refer that member to the right employee or department. Give good directions on where the person is located or point him or her out to the member, if possible.

Most members don't expect you to be an expert on all the services of your credit union, but they will expect you to know if your credit union offers a particular service and who handles it.

Give High-Quality Member Service

Credit unions are well-recognized for the quality of their member service. *American Banker* conducts and publishes annual surveys that have consistently shown that credit unions score higher than other types of financial institutions when consumers are asked about the quality of service they receive at their primary financial institution. In the 2000 survey, 79 percent of the individuals who named a credit union as their primary financial institution stated they were "very satisfied" with this choice. In the same survey, only 53 percent of consumers who use a bank as their primary financial institution were "very satisfied."

In this same survey, credit union members also expressed high satisfaction with employee courtesy, knowledge, and helpfulness in solving problems. Banks scored lower in all these measures.

Your knowledge of the credit union's services contribute to this positive perception of the quality of credit union service.

Make Cross-Sales Effectively

Your knowledge of the credit union's services helps greatly when you are trying to find solutions to member problems or ways the credit union could meet a member need. If a borrower complains that it is a nuisance to mail in loan payments, a loan employee can sell the member on automatic payment systems or other ways the member can make the payment conveniently. If the service you suggest to a member is not one you handle, you can tell the member enough information to interest him or her and then make a referral.

Compete Successfully Against Other Financial Institutions

Many of your credit union's members use the services of other financial institutions in addition to those at your credit union. They may mention features of these services that differ from how your credit union handles this type of service. The more familiar you are with your credit union's services, the more likely you will be able to point out how your credit union can offer the member advantages over the competition.

Prepare Yourself for the Future

As you work through this module, you may find you are learning about services that your credit union does not currently offer. However, learning about these services can help you prepare yourself in case your credit union does begin to offer this service. You can also more knowledgeably pass along member requests for these types of services to credit union management. In addition, if your competition offers these services, you may be able to find alternatives at your credit union that still satisfy a member's need. For example, if your credit union

---

The more familiar you are with your credit union's services, the more likely you will be able to point out how your credit union can offer the member advantages over the competition.

has a small number of ATMs, you may be able to refer members to other surcharge-free ATMs in your area.

Services Meet Member Financial Needs

The core element to all credit union services is that they meet members' financial needs. The more closely services match the members' needs, the happier members will be with the services, and the more successful you can be when encouraging members to use particular services. Therefore, before you delve deeper into the features of credit union services in this module, let's take a step back and consider the members' perspectives on credit union services.

Members come to the credit union with needs that usually fit into the following categories:

- **Need to make payments and handle daily cash flow.** Members need to be able to pay their bills conveniently, get cash when needed, and keep their daily operating funds easily accessible.
- **Need for emergency cash.** Members may quickly need funds to handle an unexpected car repair or home repair, or to bridge gaps in employment. Speed of access is critical in these situations.
- **Need to save for short-term and long-term goals.** Members may need to pay for holiday gifts, a vacation, a child's education, or retirement expenses. Down payments are also needed for large purchases such as cars and homes.
- **Need to borrow money to achieve short-term and long-term goals.** Sometimes members want to achieve a goal more quickly than would be possible by simply saving their money. Or the cost, such as for a home or car, is greater than most members could ever save to achieve. Loans and other credit are frequently used to meet these goals.
- **Need to control risk of disastrous and sudden losses.** Members need security that the monetary risk of unexpected events, such as a car accident or disability, can be controlled through insurance policies or other ways to reduce losses.

Complete activity 1.1 to analyze members' needs for financial services.

What Services Can Members Obtain at Credit Unions?

Depending on how long you have worked at your credit union, you may be more or less aware of the range of services it offers to

---

The core element to all credit union services is that they meet members' financial needs.

Member Services

INTRODUCTION TO CREDIT UNION SERVICES

Activity 1.1 Analyzing Members' Financial Needs

Match the following member statements with the type of financial need by writing the letter of the financial need on the line before each statement.

A. **Need to make payments and handle daily cash flow**
B. **Need for emergency cash**
C. **Need to save for short-term and long-term goals**
D. **Need to borrow money to achieve short-term and long-term goals**
E. **Need to control risk of disastrous and sudden losses**

_____ 1. "I'm going away to college this fall and will need to pay bills and get cash."

_____ 2. "We hope to buy a house this year."

_____ 3. "I don't know how my family would pay the bills if I wasn't around to take care of them."

_____ 4. "Now that our daughter is driving, I worry about her getting a tow or paying for a repair if the car breaks down."

_____ 5. "I really want to have money for my vacation before I go rather than pay off big bills after I get back."

Answers appear in appendix A.

---

members. However, even well-experienced employees are sometimes surprised at the number of different services that members can obtain through a credit union (or an organization owned or sponsored by the credit union). See figure 1.1 to review a list of credit union services that members can often obtain directly from a credit union or related organization. In addition, some credit unions offer even more services than what is listed here.

Savings and Transaction Accounts

The source of funds that credit unions use for making loans is the deposits in various types of

> Even well-experienced employees are sometimes surprised at the number of different services that members can obtain through a credit union

savings and transaction accounts. These accounts allow members to deposit their funds in a safe place, save for financial goals, and make transactions. Types of accounts include regular share accounts, share draft accounts, money market accounts, and share certificates. Credit unions also usually offer retirement accounts, such as individual retirement accounts (IRAs). Special "club" accounts are also often available to

7

INTRODUCTION TO CREDIT UNION SERVICES

Figure 1.1 Sample Credit Union Services

Savings and Transaction Accounts
Regular share accounts
Money market accounts
Share certificates
Retirement accounts
Share draft accounts
Savings goal accounts, such as holiday clubs and vacation clubs

Loans and Other Credit Services
Overdraft protection
Credit cards
Personal (signature) loans
Education loans
Business loans
Auto loans (and leasing)
Home purchase loans
Home equity loans (and lines of credit)

Transaction Systems
Automatic transfers
Telephone financial services
ATM cards
Debit cards
PC financial services
Electronic bill payment

Other Services
Traveler's checks
Money orders
Safe deposit boxes
Financial education
Buying services and discounts
Insurance policies
Investment services
Financial planning services

meet special savings goals. (Savings and transaction accounts are covered in chapters 2, 3, and 4.)

Loans and Other Credit Services

Loans allow members to borrow money for a variety of purposes. Members may borrow money on a short-term or long-term basis. They may also use revolving credit where the balance may go up or down. Credit cards and lines of credit are examples of revolving credit. Examples of loans and other credit services include overdraft protection, credit cards, personal (signature) loans, education loans, business loans, auto loans (and leasing), home purchase loans, and home equity loans (and lines of credit). (Loans and other credit services are covered in chapters 5 and 6.)

Transaction Systems

The traditional methods of using credit union services are to visit a branch office, make transactions by mail, or use share drafts. In addition, credit unions offer a variety of alternative systems for making transactions. These systems give members more choices in timing, location, and ease of transactions. They can make transactions when they want and how they want. Examples of transaction systems include automatic transfers (such as direct deposit and payroll deduction), telephone financial services, ATM cards, debit cards, PC financial services, and electronic bill payment. (Transaction systems are covered in chapter 7.)

Other Services

Credit unions offer members many other services depending on member needs and preferences. Some services give members additional options for making investments and protecting their funds. Other services provide members with expert advice on managing their funds and planning for the future. Credit unions provide some of these services directly; they provide others by way of a credit union service organization. Examples of other services include:

- traveler's checks
- money orders
- safe deposit boxes
- financial education (such as seminars, debt counseling, and printed materials)
- buying services and discounts
- insurance policies (such as life, credit life, credit disability, and health)
- investment services (such as annuities, mutual funds, stocks, and bonds)
- financial planning services

Services such as these are covered in chapter 8.

Complete activity 1.2 to match members' financial needs to credit union services.

How Credit Union Service Organizations (CUSOs) Provide Services to Members

Credit unions may provide services directly to members or by way of a credit union service organization. A **credit union service organization (CUSO)** is a for-profit corporation organized by a single credit union or group of credit unions. A CUSO provides operational support to credit unions or alternative financial services to members and nonmembers. Most credit unions form CUSOs for one of the following reasons:

- **To improve and support operations.** CUSOs can supply a number of support services, such as data processing and check processing, which can increase a credit union's efficiency and lower costs. For example, several credit unions may form a CUSO to provide data processing support for all the credit unions. Each credit union would have a higher cost to provide this service in-house. By forming a CUSO, the credit unions pool their resources and save money.

- **To expand financial services.** CUSOs can offer services that credit unions are not legally able to offer. By forming a CUSO, credit unions give their members access to a wider variety of services.

Member Services

INTRODUCTION TO CREDIT UNION SERVICES

Activity 1.2 Matching Member Financial Needs to Credit Union Services

Review the list of credit union services in figure 1.1 and select one or more services that match each of the following member needs. Write the name of the service(s) on the line underneath each statement.

1. "I'm going away to college this fall and will need to pay bills and get cash."

   _____

2. "We hope to buy a house this year."

   _____

3. "I don't know how my family would pay the bills if I wasn't around to take care of them."

   _____

4. "Now that our daughter is driving, I worry about her getting a tow or paying for a repair if the car breaks down."

   _____

5. "I really want to have money for my vacation before I go rather than pay off big bills after I get back."

   _____

Answers appear in appendix A.

In the area of financial services to members, CUSOs have a wide range of possibilities. Although credit unions can offer some of the following services directly, they often use CUSOs as the source for them.

- Financial planning and counseling. Financial planning is a process of assisting members to plan for a healthy and smart financial future. It usually involves educating and advising members about investment opportunities, protection plans, estate considerations, and tax considerations. It helps them map out financial goals and plans to reach them.

- Brokerage services. Members can make investments in stocks, bonds, and other choices.

- Income tax preparation. This service can assist members with completion of tax forms and filing plus tax planning.

- Real estate lending. Although some credit unions offer real estate loans directly to members, others do so

10

through a CUSO. In this way, the CUSO may originate and service loans for several credit unions and gain economies of scale.

- Travel agency services. Services include air and ground transportation, lodging, cruises, and group travel arrangements.
- Insurance. Examples of insurance include auto, health, disability, long-term care, life, property, and casualty.
- Cyber services. A CUSO can provide Internet access and web site design and hosting.

CUSOs offer qualified staff to provide these services, or they contract with outside individuals or companies. In sum, CUSOs enable many credit unions to offer services they could not otherwise offer, so it is not surprising that the number of credit unions participating in CUSOs is increasing. These for-profit organizations can tremendously help your credit union expand services to its members and streamline its own internal operations. Credit union service organizations epitomize the credit union spirit of cooperation by providing operational assistance to their credit unions and their members.

Complete activity 1.3 to find out more about CUSOs.

Activity 1.3 Does Your Credit Union Have a CUSO?

If your credit union has a CUSO, list the types of services offered.

1. Support services for the credit union?
   _____
   _____

2. Financial services for members?
   _____
   _____

3. If your credit union does not have a CUSO, what advantages might it enjoy if it formed one in the future?
   _____
   _____

Chapter 2 Opening and Administering Membership Accounts

A **credit union** is a financial cooperative organized and controlled by individuals or groups that have a common bond. Your credit union's members become owners and shareholders of the credit union when they join. Members pool their assets, providing funds for loans and other financial services to those in need within the group.

Individuals must open membership accounts to be eligible to use credit union services. The makeup of a membership account varies among credit unions, but it is typically a regular share savings account. (Types of share accounts, including regular share accounts, will be reviewed in chapter 3.)

Credit union employees need to understand several key concepts in order to open membership accounts successfully. First, a thorough understanding of the types of ownership is important so that an employee can advise members accurately. In many credit unions, the manner in which the primary or membership account is established can affect accounts the member may open in the future. In addition, your credit union and government agencies have requirements for documentation that employees must meet. After a member establishes an account, it may need to be closed for reasons such as inactivity or the death of the account owner. This chapter covers all these topics.

In addition, this chapter covers club accounts and services that credit unions offer to special membership groups.

Objectives

Upon completion of this chapter, you will be able to

1. describe the various types of account ownership, and define such terms as *joint tenancy, right of survivorship, payable on death account,* and *beneficiary;*
2. define *power of attorney* and *durable power of attorney;*
3. describe the procedures and forms necessary to process a membership application;
4. explain the credit union's responsibilities when handling decedent accounts;
5. explain how credit unions handle inactive accounts;
6. outline key features of services offered to special member groups, such as children and older members.

Individuals must open membership accounts to be eligible to use credit union services.

Types of Ownership

The ownership of an account establishes who owns the money, who can make transactions on the account, and what happens to the funds if the account owner dies. If you handle account transactions at your credit union, you need to understand account ownership to ensure you set up accounts correctly and make proper payouts of funds.

At many credit unions, potential members have a variety of ownership alternatives to choose from when they open their accounts. Popular types include sole ownership and joint ownership. In addition, credit unions often offer other types of ownerships, such as payable on death accounts or business accounts. (For more information on account ownership, see the STAR module, *S800 Opening New Accounts*.) The following section of this chapter describes a sampling of popular ownerships.

Laws regarding account ownerships vary considerably from state to state, so your credit union may have variations on the accounts described here and may also offer other ownerships. This section will use a fictitious family, the Smiths, to illustrate the general concepts of different ownership choices.

Sole Ownership

Mary Smith comes into your credit union to become a member. She opens a share account, with herself as the sole owner. As the name implies, this account is the exclusive property of Mary Smith. No other person has access to withdrawals or account information. If Mary dies, the account would become part of her estate and would be distributed according to her will or other appropriate legal document.

Joint Tenancy

Mary Smith reconsiders and decides it would be convenient if her husband, John, could make withdrawals from her account. She also wants him to receive the funds in the account quickly and easily in the event of her death. She decides to establish the account in joint tenancy, with John as joint owner. **Joint tenancy with right of survivorship (WROS)** means that each owner has equal, 100 percent access to the account and ownership of the funds. In the event of Mary's death, John would become the sole owner.

Joint tenancy accounts are available to any two or more people who wish to open a jointly owned account. Only one person must be a member of the credit union. Other types of special joint ownerships for married couples are available in some states, and you may need to learn the laws of your state to handle these accounts.

The ownership of an account establishes who owns the money, who can make transactions on the account, and what happens to the funds if the account owner dies.

Tenancy in Common

Joint tenancy should not be confused with tenancy in common. Credit unions rarely open these accounts but in case a member asks for one you need to understand the differences so that you do not mistakenly direct them to a joint tenancy account. Understanding the differences can help you see that "not all joint accounts are created alike."

In contrast to joint tenancy, a **tenancy in common** ownership gives the multiple owners ownership and access to only a portion of the account funds. The percentage of ownership for each tenant depends on the terms of the account. For example, Mary and John could each own 50 percent of the account.

An important difference between joint tenancy and tenancy in common is that tenancy in common does not have a right of survivorship. On the death of one of the owners of the tenancy in common, the deceased person's interest in the account passes to his or her estate. It does not pass to the other account tenant (unless that person is an heir of the deceased owner).

Payable on Death (POD) Accounts

A **payable on death (POD) account** is individually or jointly owned and has a designated beneficiary. The beneficiary does not have any rights or access to the funds except in the case of the death of the owner. If the account has joint owners, the beneficiary would not receive the funds until all owners have died.

For example, assume that Mary had designated John as her beneficiary. John would not be able to inquire about or make withdrawals on her account while Mary was living. He would only be able to access the funds after she died.

Or, Mary and John could own the funds jointly and designate their daughter, Clare, as beneficiary. When Mary dies, John would own the funds. When John dies, Clare would own the funds. It is common for members with children to list the children as beneficiaries.

Members without children are likely to list parents, other relatives, or friends as beneficiaries.

Payable on death account language can be written in a variety of ways. Familiarize yourself with your credit union's documents (see figure 2.1 for an example).

Other Account Ownerships

Many credit unions offer a variety of other account ownerships. Examples include:

- **custodial accounts for minors.** Members may enjoy tax advantages by setting up accounts under the **Uniform Gifts/Transfers to Minors Act,** which is available in all states. Under this state law, members set up an account ownership where an adult controls the funds but a **minor** (a person under the age of majority) owns the account. When the child reaches the age of majority, the funds must be turned over to him or her.

Figure 2.1 Sample Payable on Death Agreement

```
PAYMENT ON DEATH AGREEMENT - SINGLE ACCOUNT
          HEARTLAND CREDIT UNION
Member Name _____
              Last          First           MI

Certificate of Deposit No. _____  Account No. _____

I, the undersigned, hereby authorize and direct Heartland Credit Union to pay,
upon my death, any and all amounts then credited to the Certificate of Deposit
or account specified above to:
_____
_____
                                              (beneficiary/ies)
If more than one beneficiary is named, those living upon my death shall equally
share the proceeds of this account or Certificate of Deposit.

Provided, however, that such payment shall be subject to the bylaws and
amendments thereto of the credit union, any restrictions or limitations imposed
by applicable law, and any right which the credit union may have to apply
amounts now or hereafter credited to such account or Certificate of Deposit to
the payment of any indebtedness which I now have or may then have to the
credit union.

Signed this _____ day of _____, 20___

This account/Certificate of Deposit is owned by the party named hereon,
upon the death of any of such party, ownership passes to the P.O.D.
beneficiary(ies) named hereon.

_____
WITNESS

_____   _____
WITNESS                SIGNATURE OF MEMBER
```

Source: © Heartland Credit Union, Madison, Wisconsin. Reprinted with permission.

- **organization accounts.** Local non profit groups such as clubs, charities, or other groups can open accounts in the ownership of the organization.
- **business accounts.** Credit unions may open accounts for corporations, partnerships, and other businesses in the name of the business. Usually, the owner(s) or officers of the business have the authority to conduct transactions. The account continues even if the business changes the authorized signers.

Credit unions can set up ownership of a member's account in a number of different ways. The differences among these alternatives, although they might seem insignificant at the time the account is established, can make a tremendous difference if the member's circumstances change (through marriage, divorce, or death, for example). Be aware of what your credit union's ownership alternatives are under your state's laws and be prepared to explain them completely and accurately to members.

Consider the differences among joint tenancy, tenancy in common, and payable on death accounts by completing activity 2.1

Power of Attorney

Although not an account ownership, power of attorney is explained here because it affects who can make transactions on an account. A **power of attorney** is a document authorizing a person or persons to make withdrawals from an account and conduct any other authorized transactions on behalf of that individual. The person so authorized does not have to be an attorney. The owner of the account signs the document authorizing the named person to act legally on his or her behalf under certain conditions and for specific purposes. The person granted the power of attorney also signs the document. This document does not affect any of the owner's rights.

Activity 2.1 Comparing Account Ownerships

Fill in the appropriate provisions for each of the following types of accounts.

Type of Account Ownership	How do Sean and Rebecca own the money?	What happens to the money if Rebecca dies?
Sean and Rebecca (joint tenants WROS)		
Sean and Rebecca (tenants in common)		
Sean and Rebecca (POD to Tara)		

Answers appear in appendix A.

A power of attorney can authorize a named person to conduct transactions and make decisions for a person in addition to management of a particular account. A credit union member may want to create a power of attorney giving someone legal authority to sell real estate for him in his absence. Or a member who is unable to write (perhaps due to illness) may give someone power of attorney so share drafts can be made out and bills paid. These are just two examples of situations that may occur at any time in your credit union.

The power of attorney can be indefinite or have a limited and specific term set out in the document itself. In either case, the member/owner can revoke or change the power of attorney by advising the credit union in writing. A power of attorney is automatically cancelled on the member/owner's death.

A power of attorney may also be cancelled on the incapacity of the member/owner or it can continue depending on how the power of attorney document is written. If the member/owner has signed what is called a **durable power of attorney,** then it will continue even if the member/owner is incapacitated and no longer able to make financial decisions. For example, a member/owner may have authorized a durable power of attorney before a serious operation that results in a coma. The person holding the power of attorney has the right to continue to take authorized actions while the member/owner is in the coma. However, this type of power of attorney is still cancelled on the death of the member/owner.

You need to learn about power of attorney if you handle account transactions for members. Learn your credit union's procedures for accepting a power of attorney and allowing transactions.

Account Documentation

Opening new accounts calls for a variety of documentation. The prospective member furnishes information to the credit union and the credit union must also furnish information to the new member. Following is a list of the primary documents typically involved in a new membership account:

- membership application;
- account agreement;
- signature card;
- account disclosures;
- membership identification card.

Membership Application

Many credit unions require potential members to complete an application when joining. See figure 2.2 for an example of an application that can be downloaded from a credit union's web site. (Credit union web sites are explained in chapter 7.) The membership application requests all the pertinent information about a prospective member (and potential borrower) and, therefore, needs to be completed fully and accurately. For example, the application asks the member to furnish a tax identification number, which is often the social security number. This number is a form of account verification. The credit union could be penalized by the federal government if it does not obtain this number in a timely manner.

The information on the membership application has other uses, also. Often this information is used to pre-approve new members for signature or line-of-credit loans. The membership application also gives valuable information about the new member that may indicate needs for other products and services.

Account Agreement

An account agreement may be part of the membership application or presented as a separate document. The account agreement spells out many of the terms and conditions that make up the account contract between the member and the credit union. A **contract** is a binding written agreement between two or more parties enforceable by law. The elements of the account contract between the member and the credit union are primarily spelled out in

- state and federal laws;
- state and federal regulations;
- the credit union's bylaws and policies;
- credit union account records;
- account signature cards;
- the account agreement provided by the credit union.

Figure 2.2 Sample Membership Application

| Last Name | First Name | Middle Initial | Account # |

MEMBERSHIP ENROLLMENT & UNIVERSAL APPLICATION

Please provide the following information. When you have completed the form, print and mail your application with any money owed to Xerox Federal Credit Union for processing. See step 8 for delivery information.

Step 1) Fill out Membership Application

Membership Application

MEMBERSHIP INFORMATION

Qualification for Membership:
- ☐ Xerox Employee ☐ Xerox Retiree ☐ Xerox Affiliate/Supplier
- ☐ Spouse, Roommate, or Relative of one of the above
  Spouse/Roommate/Relative's Information: Name:
  Account Number:
  Relationship:
  Phone #:

Your Name
Street Address
City   State   Zip Code
Home Phone # ( ) -   Date of Birth
Mother's Maiden Name
Social Security Number   -   -
Driver's License #:   State:
Employee Badge #:

EMPLOYER INFORMATION

Employer's Name   Position
Street Address   City   State   Zip
Outside Phone # ( ) -   ext.   Hire Date

MEMBERSHIP ACCOUNT

Membership Requirement – Maintain a $5 minimum balance in a Regular Savings Account)
Membership Savings Account
    Initial Deposit $ _____
    ($5.00 minimum to enroll, $100.00 minimum balance to earn dividends, $100.00 minimum total balance of all accounts)

Source: © Xerox Federal Credit Union, El Segundo, California. Reprinted with permission.

Member Services

OPENING AND ADMINISTERING MEMBERSHIP ACCOUNTS

Figure 2.2 Sample Membership Application (Continued)

Step 2) <u>Indicate Joint Owners</u>, skip if none

JOINT OWNERS

Joint Owner (1) Name　　Social Security # ‑ ‑
Street Address　　Date of Birth / /
City　　State　　Zip Code
Home Phone # (　)　　Work Phone # (　)　　ext.
Mother's Maiden Name
Driver's License #:　　State:
Signature X_____
Add joint owner to: ☐ Savings ☐ Checking ☐ Club ☐ PMMA ☐ CMMA ☐ Certificate

Joint Owner (2) Name　　Social Security # ‑ ‑
Street Address　　Date of Birth / /
City　　State　　Zip Code
Home Phone # (　)　　Work Phone # (　)　　ext.
Mother's Maiden Name
Driver's License #:　　State:
Signature X_____
Add joint owner to: ☐ Savings ☐ Checking ☐ Club ☐ PMMA ☐ CMMA ☐ Certificate

Step 3) <u>Indicate Beneficiary Information</u>, skip if none

BENEFICIARY INFORMATION

Upon my and all joint owner's death, pay all sums to:
Social Security # ‑ ‑　　Relationship:
Add beneficiary to: ☐ Savings ☐ Checking ☐ Club ☐ PMMA ☐ CMMA ☐ Certificate
Upon my and all joint owner's death, pay all sums to:
Social Security # ‑ ‑　　Relationship:
Add beneficiary to: ☐ Savings ☐ Checking ☐ Club ☐ PMMA ☐ CMMA ☐ Certificate

Figure 2.2 Sample Membership Application (Continued)

Step 4) Apply for Accounts, skip if just applying for membership

APPLICATION FOR ACCOUNTS

Checking Accounts

☐ *Regular Checking* (no minimum balance)
    Initial Deposit $ (Initial Deposit of $100.00 or Direct Deposit of your net check.)
☐ *Checking Plus* (interest-bearing; $2,000.00 minimum balance)
    Initial Deposit $ (Initial Deposit of $2,000.00)

    ☐ *Free** Check Order*
    (**first box of checks when opened with Direct Deposit; corporate image style only)
    For checks other than the corporate image style, visit our web site at www.xfcu.org, see a Xerox Federal Credit Union Representative, or call TeleServices at (800) XFCU-222 Monday thru Friday, 6AM to 6PM Pacific Time, 7AM to 7PM Mountain Time, 8AM to 8PM Central Time, 9AM to 9PM Eastern Time.

    In addition to my name and address, please include the following on my checks:
    ^Phone # ( ) -
    ^My Driver's License #:
    ^Joint Owner:
    ^Joint Owner's Driver's License #:
    ^Information is optional

    ☐ *Overdraft Protection (recommended for your checking account)*
    I hereby authorize Xerox Federal Credit Union to pay overdrafts on my checking account from my other XFCU accounts. Out of the 4 options to choose from for my overdraft path, I choose the following option (check one):

        ☐ Regular Savings only (3 per month)
        ☐ PowerLine of Credit Loan only (unlimited)
        ☐ Regular Savings first, if savings funds are not available then debit from PowerLine of Credit (PLOC)
        ☐ PowerLine of Credit (PLOC) first, if PLOC funds are not available then debit from Regular Savings

☐ *Club Account*
Initial Deposit #1 $ *($5.00 minimum balance per account)*
Personalized Account Name (#1)

Initial Deposit #2 $ *($5.00 minimum balance per account)*
Personalized Account Name (#2)

☐ *Prime Money Market Account (PMMA)*
Initial Deposit $ ($1,000 minimum balance.)
    ☐ Please order my free supply of 50 checks *(Restrictions: only 3 checks may clear per month)*

☐ *Capital Money Market Account (CMMA)*
Initial Deposit $ ($15,000 minimum balance)

☐ *Certificates*
Select from list: Bronze, 6 Months, $1,000 minimum balance   Initial Deposit $
Initial Deposit $

☐ *Retirement Accounts*

OPENING AND ADMINISTERING MEMBERSHIP ACCOUNTS

Figure 2.2 Sample Membership Application (Continued)

Step 5) Apply for Automated Services, skip if none

APPLICATION FOR SERVICES

The following services give you anytime, anywhere access to your accounts. Simply initial next to the free service(s) you would like to have, and a Personal Identification Number and card/software will be mailed to you.

☐ *XFCU Visa Check Card* (Checking account required.)
please initial: _____
Additional card for Joint Owner (optional) -Name

☐ *XFCU ATM CashCard*   Please initial: _____
Additional card for Joint Owner (optional) -Name

☐ *SuperAxcess Web Banking*   Please initial: _____

Step 6) Fill out Certification Information, (indicate withholding status)

CERTIFICATION INFORMATION

I certify that the number shown on this form is my correct social security number/tax identification number and that:
(please check one of the following boxes)

☐ I am not subject to backup withholding under the provisions of section 3405(a)(1)(C) of the Internal Revenue Code.
☐ I am subject to backup withholding

I agree to conform to the Xerox Federal Credit Union bylaws and "Agreement and Truth in Savings Disclosures" and any amendments thereto, I agree to abide by the terms and conditions of the "Electronic Services Disclosures and Agreement" and any amendments thereto. Also, by signing below, I authorize you to check my credit and employment history and to release information regarding status and history of my account(s) to other creditors. Any information obtained from consumer reporting agencies will not be sold to outside parties, and will be used only in conjunction with products offered by XFCU.

Under the penalties of perjury, I certify that the information provided on this card is true, correct, and complete.

Member/Owner Signature X_____   Date _____

Step 7) Print and Sign Application

Step 8) Mail application, and send any money owed*, to:

Xerox Federal Credit Union
Attn: Member Services
2200 E. Grand Avenue
El Segundo, CA 90245

* Membership becomes effective when deposit is received.

Figure 2.2 Sample Membership Application (Continued)

Step 9: Apply for a Loan†
(necessary if you indicated PowerLine of Credit for overdraft protection, and do not have one).

† The Loan Application can be completed online in the XFCU web site at **http://www.xfcu.org**. Also, versions of the application are available at this site for downloading to your hard drive, printing and filing manually.

Please be advised that while Xerox Federal Credit Union provides services and products to Xerox employees and their families, the Credit Union is a separate legal entity and is neither owned nor controlled by Xerox Corporation. Further the Credit Union subsidiary, XCU Capital Corp., is neither owned nor controlled by Xerox Corporation. Xerox Corporation does not endorse nor recommend any product or service that the Credit Union or XCU Capital Corp. Inc., sells or makes available to Xerox employees and their families. You are strongly urged to consult a financial advisor before making any investment decision.

For Office Use Only - Please Do Not Write in Box

Opened: ☐ Savings ☐ Checking ☐ Club ☐ PMMA ☐ CMMA
Ordered: ☐ Checking Account Checks ☐ PMMA Checks
☐ Axcess Kit ☐ Visa Check Card ☐ ATM CashCard ☐ **Chex Systems**

Application Received: **Rep. Name:** **Initials:**
Membership Officer:

The credit union gives a copy of the account agreement to the member when he or she joins. The account agreement discloses many of the rules of the account, such as

- information about different ownership types and rules;
- how the credit union determines who can withdraw from an account;
- any restrictions on withdrawals;
- rules for honoring checks or drafts;
- authorization to the credit union to provide a member's endorsement if it is missing from a check deposited to the account;
- requirements on how to notify the credit union about errors;
- what happens to funds in the account in the event of the member's death.

Figure 2.3 is an example of an account agreement.

Member Services

OPENING AND ADMINISTERING MEMBERSHIP ACCOUNTS

Figure 2.3 Sample Account Agreement

MEMBERSHIP AND ACCOUNT AGREEMENT

This Agreement covers your and our rights and responsibilities concerning Accounts the Credit Union (Credit Union) offers. In this Agreement, the words "you" and "yours" mean anyone who signs an Account Card or Account Change Card (Account Card). The words "we," "us," and "our" mean the Credit Union. The word "account" means any one or more share or other accounts you have with the Credit Union.

Your account type(s) and ownership features are designated on your Account Card. By signing an Account Card, each of you, jointly and severally, agree to the terms and conditions in this Agreement and Account Card, the Funds Availability Policy Disclosure, Truth-in-Savings Rate and Fee Schedule (Rate and Fee Schedule), and any Account Receipt accompanying this Agreement, and the Credit Union's Bylaws and policies, and any amendments to these documents from time to time which collectively govern your Membership and Accounts.

1. **Membership Eligibility.** To join the Credit Union you must meet the membership requirements including purchase and maintenance of at least one (1) share ("membership share") as set forth in the Credit Union's Bylaws. You authorize us to check your account, credit, and employment history, and obtain reports from third parties, including credit reporting agencies, to verify your eligibility for the accounts and services you request.

2. **Single Party Accounts.** A single party account is an account owned by one member (individual, corporation, partnership, trust or other organization) qualified for credit union membership. If the account owner dies, the interest passes, subject to applicable law, to the decedent's estate or Payable on Death (POD) beneficiary/payee or trust beneficiary, subject to other provisions of this Agreement governing our protection for honoring transfer and withdrawal requests of an owner or owner's agent prior to notice of an owner's death.

3. **Multiple Party Accounts.** An account owned by two or more persons is a multiple party account.

   a. Rights of Survivorship. Unless otherwise stated on the Account Card, a multiple party account includes rights of survivorship. This means when one owner dies, all sums in the account will pass to the surviving owner(s). For a multiple party account without rights of survivorship, the deceased owner's interest passes to his or her estate. A surviving owner's interest is subject to the Credit Union's statutory lien for the deceased owner's obligations, and to any security interest or pledge granted by a deceased owner, even if a surviving owner did not consent to it.

   b. Control of Multiple Party Accounts. Any owner is authorized and deemed to act for any other owner(s) and may instruct us regarding transactions and other account matters. Each owner guarantees the signature of any other owner(s). Any owner may withdraw all funds, stop payment on items, transfer, or pledge to us all or any part of the shares without the consent of the other owner(s). We have no duty to notify any owner(s) about any transaction. We reserve the right to require written consent of all owners for any change to or termination of an account. If we receive written notice of a dispute between owners or inconsistent instructions from them, we may suspend or terminate the account and require a court order or written consent from all owners to act.

   c. Multiple Party Account Owner Liability. If a deposited item in a multiple party account is returned unpaid, an account is overdrawn, or if we do not receive final payment on a transaction, the owners, jointly and severally, are liable to us for the amount of the returned item, overdraft, or unpaid amount and any charges, regardless of who initiated or benefited from the transaction. If any account owner is indebted to us, we may enforce our rights against any account of an owner or all funds in the multiple party account regardless of who contributed them.

4. **POD/Trust Account Designations.** A Payable on Death (POD) account or trust account designation is an instruction to the Credit Union that a single or multiple party account so designated is payable to the owner(s) during his, her or their lifetimes and, when the last account owner dies, payable to any named and surviving POD or trust beneficiary/payee. Accounts payable to more than one surviving beneficiary/payee are owned jointly by such beneficiaries/payees without rights of survivorship. Any POD or trust beneficiary/payee designation shall not apply to Individual Retirement Accounts (IRAs) which are governed by a separate beneficiary/payee designation. We are not obligated to notify any beneficiary/payee of the existence of any account or the vesting of the beneficiary/payee's interest in any account, except as otherwise provided by law.

5. **Accounts for Minors.** We may require any account established by a minor to be a multiple party account with an owner who has reached the age of majority under state law and who shall be jointly and severally liable to us for any returned item, overdraft, or unpaid charges or amounts on such account. We may pay funds directly to the minor without regard to his or her minority. Unless a guardian or parent is an account owner, the guardian or parent shall not have any account access rights. We have no duty to inquire about the use or purpose of any transaction. We will not change the account status when the minor reaches the age of majority, unless authorized in writing by all account owners.

6. **Uniform Transfers/Gifts to Minors Account.** A Uniform Transfers/Gifts to Minors Account (UTTMA/UGMA) is an individual account created by a custodian who deposits funds as an irrevocable gift to a minor. The minor to whom the gift is made is the beneficiary of the custodial property in the account. The custodian has possession and control of the account for the exclusive right and benefit of the minor and barring a court order otherwise, is the only party entitled to make deposits, withdrawals, or close the account. We have no duty to inquire about the use or purpose of any transaction. If the custodian dies, we may suspend the account, until we receive instructions from any person authorized by law to withdraw funds or a court order authorizing withdrawal.

7. **Agency Designation on an Account.** An agency designation on an account is an instruction to us that the owner authorizes another person to make transactions as agent for the account owner regarding the accounts designated. An agent has no ownership interest in the account(s) or Credit Union voting rights. We have no duty to inquire about the use or purpose of any transaction made by the agent.

8. **Deposit of Funds Requirements.** Funds may be deposited to any account, in any manner approved by the Credit Union in accordance with the requirements set forth on the Rate and Fee Schedule.

   a. Endorsements. We may accept transfers, checks, drafts, and other items for deposit into any of your accounts if they are made payable to, or to the order of, one or more account owners even if they are not endorsed by all payees. You authorize us to supply missing endorsements of any owners if we choose. If a check, draft or item that is payable to two or more persons is ambiguous as to whether it is payable to either or both, we may process the check, draft or item as though it is payable to either person. If an insurance, government, or other check or draft requires an endorsement as set forth on the back of the check or draft, we may require endorsements as set forth on the item. Endorsements must be made on the back of the share draft or check within 1½ inches from the top edge, although we may accept endorsements outside this space. However, any loss we incur from a delay or processing error resulting from an irregular endorsement or other markings by you or any prior endorser will be your responsibility.

   b. Collection of Items. We act only as your agent and we are not responsible for handling items for deposit or collection beyond the exercise of ordinary care. Deposits made by mail or at unstaffed facilities are not our responsibility until we receive them. We are not liable for the negligence of any correspondent or for loss in transit, and each correspondent will only be liable for its own negligence. We may send any item for collection. Items drawn on an institution located outside the United States are handled on a collection basis only. You waive any notice of nonpayment, dishonor, or protest regarding items we purchase or receive for credit or collection to your account.

   c. Final Payment. All items or Automated Clearing House (ACH) transfers credited to your account are provisional until we receive final payment. If final payment is not received, we may charge your account for the amount of such items or ACH transfers and impose a return item charge on your account. Any collection fees we incur may be charged to your account. We reserve the right to refuse or return any item or funds transfer.

   d. Direct Deposits. We may offer preauthorized deposits (e.g., payroll checks, Social Security or retirement checks, or other government checks) or preauthorized transfers from other accounts. You must authorize each direct deposit or preauthorized transfer by filling out a separate form. You

Source: © CUNA Mutual Operational Forms

Figure 2.3 Sample Account Agreement (Continued)

must notify us at least thirty (30) days in advance to cancel or change a direct deposit or transfer option. Upon a bankruptcy filing, unless you cancel an authorization we will continue making direct deposits in accordance with your authorization on file with us. If we are required to reimburse the U.S. Government for any benefit payment directly deposited into your account, we may deduct the amount returned from any of your accounts, unless prohibited by law.

e. Crediting of Deposits. Deposits made after the deposit cutoff time and deposits made on either holidays or days that are not our business days will be credited to your account on the next business day.

9. Account Access.

a. Authorized Signature. Your signature on the Account Card authorizes your account access. We will not be liable for refusing to honor any item or instruction if we believe the signature is not genuine. If you have authorized the use of a facsimile signature, we may honor any draft that appears to bear your facsimile signature even if it was made by an unauthorized person. You authorize us to honor transactions initiated by a third person to whom you have given your account number even if you do not authorize a particular transaction.

b. Access Options. You may withdraw or transfer funds from your account(s) in any manner we permit (e.g., at an automated teller machine, in person, by mail, automatic transfer, or telephone, as applicable). We may return as unpaid any draft drawn on a form we do not provide, and you are responsible for any loss we incur handling such a draft. We have the right to review and approve any form of power of attorney and may restrict account withdrawals or transfers. We are under no obligation to honor any power of attorney.

c. ACH & Wire Transfers. If we provide the service, you may initiate or receive credits or debits to your account through wire or ACH transfer. You agree that if you receive funds by a wire or ACH transfer, we are not required to notify you at the time the funds are received. Instead, the transfer will be shown on your periodic statement. We may provisionally credit your account for an ACH transfer before we receive final settlement. We may reverse the provisional credit or you will refund us the amount if we do not receive final settlement. When you initiate a wire transfer, you may identify either the recipient or any financial institution by name and by account or identifying number. The Credit Union (and other institutions) may rely on the account or other identifying number as the proper identification even if it identifies a different party or institution.

d. Credit Union Examination. We may disregard information on any draft or check, other than the signature of the drawer, the amount and any magnetic encoding. You agree we do not fail to exercise ordinary care in paying an item solely because our procedures do not provide for sight examination of items.

10. Account Rates and Fees. We pay account earnings and assess fees against your account as set forth in the Rate and Fee Schedule. We may change the Rate and Fee Schedule at any time and will notify you as required by law.

11. Transaction Limitations.

a. Withdrawal Restrictions. We permit withdrawals only if your account has sufficient available funds to cover the full amount of the withdrawal or you have an established overdraft protection plan. Drafts or other transfer or payment orders which are drawn against insufficient funds may be subject to a service charge set forth in the Rate and Fee Schedule. If there are sufficient funds to cover some, but not all, of your withdrawal, we may allow those withdrawals for which there are sufficient funds in any order at our discretion.

We may refuse to allow a withdrawal in some situations, and will advise you accordingly; for example: (1) a dispute between account owners (unless a court has ordered the Credit Union to allow the withdrawal); (2) a legal garnishment or attachment is served; (3) the account secures any obligation to us; (4) required documentation has not been presented; (5) you fail to repay a Credit Union loan on time. We may require you to give written notice of seven (7) days to sixty (60) days before any intended withdrawals.

b. Transfer Limitations. For share savings and money market accounts, if applicable, you may make up to six (6) preauthorized, automatic, telephonic, or audio response transfers to another account of yours or to a third party during any calendar month. Of these six, you may make no more than three (3) transfers to a third party by check or debit card. A preauthorized transfer includes any arrangement with us to pay a third party from your account upon oral or written orders including orders received through the automated clearing house (ACH). You may make unlimited transfers to any of your accounts or to any Credit Union loan account and may make withdrawals in person, by mail, or at an ATM. However, we may refuse or reverse a transfer that exceeds these limitations and may assess fees against, suspend or close your account.

12. Certificate Accounts. Any time deposit, term share, share certificate, or certificate of deposit account allowed by state law (Certificate Account), whichever we offer, is subject to the terms of this Agreement, the Rate and Fee Schedule and Account Deposit Receipt for each account the terms of which are incorporated herein by reference.

13. Overdrafts.

a. Overdraft Liability. If on any day, the funds in your share account are not sufficient to cover drafts, fees or other items posted to your account, those amounts will be handled in accordance with our overdraft procedures or an overdraft protection plan you have with us. The Credit Union's determination of an insufficient account balance may be made at any time between presentation and the Credit Union's midnight deadline with only one review of the account required. We do not have to notify you if your account does not have funds to cover drafts, fees or other posted items. Whether the item is paid or returned, your account may be subject to a charge as set forth in the Rate and Fee Schedule. Except as otherwise agreed in writing, we, by covering one or any overdraft, do not agree to cover overdrafts in the future and may discontinue covering overdrafts at any time without notice. If we pay a draft or impose a fee that would otherwise overdraw your account, you agree to pay the overdrawn amount immediately. We reserve the right to pursue collection of previously dishonored items at any time, including giving a payor bank extra time beyond any midnight deadline limits.

b. Overdraft Protection Plan. If we have approved an overdraft protection plan for your account, we will honor drafts drawn on insufficient funds by transferring funds from another account under this Agreement or a loan account, as you have directed, or as required under the Credit Union's overdraft protection policy. The fee for overdraft transfers, if any, is set forth on the Rate and Fee Schedule. This Agreement governs all transfers, except those governed by agreements for loan accounts.

14. Postdated and Staledated Drafts. We may pay any draft without regard to its date unless you notify us of a postdating. The notice must be given to us in time so that we can notify our employees and reasonably act upon the notice and must accurately describe the draft, including the exact number, date, and amount. You understand that the exact information is necessary for the Credit Union's computer to identify the draft. We are not responsible if you give us an incorrect or incomplete description, or untimely notice. You may make an oral notice which lapses in fourteen (14) calendar days unless confirmed in writing. A written notice is effective for six (6) months and may be renewed in writing from time to time. You agree not to deposit checks, drafts, or other items before they are properly payable. We are not obligated to pay any check or draft drawn on your account which is presented more than six (6) months past its date.

15. Stop Payment Orders.

a. Stop Payment Order Request. You may request a stop payment order on any draft drawn on your account. To be binding an order must be dated, signed, and describe the account and draft number and the exact amount. The stop payment will be effective if the Credit Union receives the order in time for the Credit Union to act upon the order and you state the number of the account, number of the draft, and its exact amount. You understand that the exact information is necessary for the Credit Union's computer to identify the draft. If you give us incorrect or incomplete information, we will not be responsible for failing to stop payment on the draft. If the stop payment order is not received in time for us to act upon the order, we will not be liable to you or to any other party for payment of the draft. If we recredit your account after paying a draft over a valid and timely stop payment order, you agree to sign a statement describing the

b. Duration of Order. You may make an oral stop payment order which will lapse within fourteen (14) calendar days unless confirmed in writing within that time. A written stop payment order is effective for six (6) months and may be renewed in writing from time to time. We do not have to notify you when a stop payment order expires.

c. Liability. Fees for stop payment orders are set forth on the Rate and Fee Schedule. You may not stop payment on any certified check, cashier's check, teller's check, or any other check, draft, or payment guaranteed by us. Although payment of an item may be stopped, you may remain liable to any item holder, including us. You agree to indemnify and hold the Credit Union harmless from all costs, including attorney's fees, damages or claims related to our refusing payment of an item, including claims of any multiple party account owner, payee, or indorsee in failing to stop payment of an item as a result of incorrect information provided by you.

16. Credit Union Liability. If we do not properly complete a transaction according to this Agreement, we will be liable for your losses or damages not to exceed the amount of the transaction, except as otherwise provided by law. We will not be liable if: (1) your account contains insufficient funds for the transaction; (2) circumstances beyond our control prevent the transaction; (3) your loss is caused by your or another financial institution's negligence; or (4) your account funds are subject to legal process or other claim. We will not be liable for consequential damages, except liability for wrongful dishonor. We exercise ordinary care if our actions or nonactions are consistent with applicable state law, federal reserve regulations and operating letters, clearinghouse rules, and general banking practices followed in the area we serve. You grant us the right, in making payments of deposited funds, to rely exclusively on the form of the account and the terms of this Account Agreement. Any conflict between what you or our employees may say or write will be resolved by reference to this Agreement.

17. Credit Union Lien and Security Interest. If you owe us money as a borrower, guarantor, endorser or otherwise, we have a lien on the account funds in any account in which you have an ownership interest, regardless of their source, unless prohibited by law. We may apply these funds in any order to pay off your indebtedness. By not enforcing a lien, we do not waive our right to enforce it later. In addition, you grant the Credit Union a consensual security interest in your accounts and we may use the funds from your accounts to pay any debt or amount now or hereafter owed the Credit Union, except for obligations secured by your residence, unless prohibited by applicable law. All accounts are nonassignable and nontransferable to third parties.

18. Legal Process. If any legal action is brought against your account, we may pay out funds according to the terms of the action or refuse any payout until the dispute is resolved. Any expenses or attorney fees we incur responding to legal process may be charged against your account without notice, unless prohibited by law. Any legal process against your account is subject to our lien and security interest.

19. Account Information. Upon request, we will give you the name and address of each agency from which we obtain a credit report regarding your account. We agree not to disclose account information to third parties except when: (1) it is necessary to complete a transaction; (2) the third party seeks to verify the existence or condition of your account in accordance with applicable law; (3) such disclosure complies with the law or a government agency or court order; or (4) you give us written permission.

20. Notices.

a. Name or Address Changes. You are responsible for notifying us of any address or name change. The Credit Union is only required to attempt to communicate with you at the most recent address you have provided to us. We may accept oral notices of a change in address and may require any other notice from you to us be provided in writing. If we attempt to locate you, we may impose a service fee as set forth on the Rate and Fee Schedule.

b. Notice of Amendments. Except as prohibited by applicable law, we may change the terms of this Agreement. We will notify you of any changes in terms, rates, or fees as required by law. We reserve the right to waive

Member Services

OPENING AND ADMINISTERING MEMBERSHIP ACCOUNTS

Figure 2.3 Sample Account Agreement (Continued)

any term in this Agreement. Any such waiver shall not affect our right to future enforcement.

c. **Effect of Notice.** Any written notice you give us is effective when we receive it. Any written notice we give to you is effective when it is deposited in the U.S. Mail, postage prepaid and addressed to you at your statement mailing address. Notice to any account owner is considered notice to all account owners.

21. **Taxpayer Identification Numbers and Backup Withholding.** Your failure to furnish a correct Taxpayer Identification Number (TIN) or meet other requirements may result in backup withholding. If your account is subject to backup withholding, we must withhold and pay to the Internal Revenue Service (IRS) a percentage of dividends, interest, and certain other payments. If you fail to provide your TIN, we may suspend opening your account, or, if applicable, you may request a non-dividend or non-interest bearing account until a TIN is provided.

22. **Statements.**

a. **Contents.** If we provide a periodic statement for your account, you will receive a periodic statement of transactions and activity on your account during the statement period as required by applicable law. If a periodic statement is provided, you agree that only one statement is necessary for a multiple party account. For share draft or checking accounts, you understand and agree that your original draft, when paid, becomes property of the Credit Union and may not be returned to you, but copies may be retained by us or payable through financial institutions and made available upon your request. You understand and agree that statements are made available to you on the date they are mailed to you. You also understand and agree that drafts or copies thereof are made available to you on the date the statement is mailed to you, even if the drafts do not accompany the statement.

b. **Examination.** You are responsible for examining each statement and reporting any irregularities to us. We will not be responsible for any forged, altered, unauthorized or unsigned items drawn on your account if: (1) you fail to notify us within thirty-three (33) days of the mailing date of the earliest statement regarding any forgery, alteration or unauthorized signature on any item described in the statement; or (2) any items are forged or altered in a manner not detectable by a reasonable person, including the unauthorized use of a facsimile signature machine.

c. **Notice to Credit Union.** You agree that the Credit Union's retention of drafts does not alter or waive your responsibility to examine your statements or the time limit for notifying us of any errors. The statement will be considered correct for all purposes and we will not be liable for any payment made or charge to your account unless you notify us in writing within the above time limit for notifying us of any errors. If you fail to receive a periodic statement you agree to notify us within fourteen (14) days of the time you regularly receive a statement.

23. **Inactive Accounts.** If your account falls below any applicable minimum balance and you have not made any transactions over a period specified in the Rate and Fee Schedule during which we have been unable to contact you by regular mail, we may classify your account as inactive or dormant. Unless prohibited by applicable law, we may charge a service fee set forth on the Rate and Fee Schedule for processing your inactive account. If we impose a fee, we will notify you, as required by law, at your last known address. You authorize us to transfer funds from another account of yours to cover any service fees, if applicable. To the extent allowed by law, we reserve the right to suspend any further account statements. If a deposit or withdrawal has not been made on the account and we have had no other sufficient contact with you within the period specified by state law, the account will be presumed to be abandoned. Funds in abandoned accounts will be reported and remitted in accordance with state law. Once funds have been turned over to the state, we have no further liability to you for such funds and if you choose to reclaim such funds, you must apply to the appropriate state agency.

24. **Special Account Instructions.** You may request that we facilitate certain trust, will, or court-ordered account arrangements. However, because we do not give legal advice, we cannot counsel you as to which account arrangement most appropriately meets the specific requirements of your trust, will, or court order. If you ask us to follow any instructions

that we believe might expose us to claims, lawsuits, expenses, liabilities, or damages, whether directly or indirectly, we may refuse to follow your instructions or may require you to indemnify us or post a bond or provide us with other protection. Account changes requested by you, or any account owner, such as adding or closing an account or service, must be evidenced by a signed Account Change form and accepted by us.

25. **Termination of Account.** We may terminate your account at any time without notice to you or may require you to close your account and apply for a new account if: (1) there is a change in owners or authorized signers; (2) there has been a forgery or fraud reported or committed involving your account; (3) there is a dispute as to the ownership of the account or of the funds in the account; (4) any share drafts are lost or stolen; (5) there are excessive returned unpaid items not covered by an overdraft protection plan; (6) there has been any misrepresentation or any other abuse of any of your accounts; or (7) we reasonably deem it necessary to prevent a loss to us. You may terminate a single party account by giving written notice. We reserve the right to require the consent of all owners to terminate a multiple party account. We are not responsible for payment of any draft, withdrawal, or other item after your account is terminated, however, if we pay an item after termination, you agree to reimburse us.

26. **Termination of Membership.** You may terminate your membership by giving us notice. You may be denied services or expelled for any reason allowed by applicable law, including causing a loss to the Credit Union.

27. **Death of Account Owner.** We may continue to honor all transfer orders, withdrawals, deposits and other transactions on an account until we are notified of a member's death. Once we are notified of a member's death, we may pay drafts or honor other payments or transfer orders authorized by the deceased member for a period of ten (10) days after that date unless we receive instructions from any person claiming an interest in the account to stop payment on the drafts or other items. We may require anyone claiming a deceased owner's account funds to indemnify us for any losses resulting from our honoring that claim. This Agreement will be binding upon any heirs or legal representatives of any account owner.

28. **Severability.** If a court holds any portion of this Agreement to be invalid or unenforceable, the remainder of this Agreement shall not be invalid or unenforceable and will continue in full force and effect. All headings are intended for reference only and are not to be construed as part of the Agreement.

29. **Enforcement.** You are liable to us for any loss, cost or expense we incur resulting from your failure to follow this Agreement. You authorize us to deduct any such loss, costs or expenses from your account without prior notice to you. If we bring a legal action to collect any amount due under or to enforce this Agreement, we shall be entitled, subject to applicable law, to payment of reasonable attorney's fees and costs, including fees on any appeal, bankruptcy proceedings, and any post-judgment collection actions.

30. **Governing Law.** This Agreement is governed by the Credit Union's Bylaws, federal laws and regulations, the laws, including applicable principles of contract law, and regulations of the state in which the Credit Union's main office is located, and local clearinghouse rules, as amended from time to time. As permitted by applicable law, you agree that any legal action regarding this Agreement shall be brought in the county in which the Credit Union is located.

Source: © Copyright CUNA Service Group, Inc., Reprinted with permission

Signature Card

At many credit unions, the member completes a separate signature card when opening an account. The card may include parts of the account contract and may refer to a separate account agreement for additional terms. The card also usually sets out the specific type of ownership for the account. By signing the card, the member signifies acceptance of the terms of the account contract and provides a specimen signature. All the account owners sign the card; the credit union may later use the card to verify signatures on transactions.

Account Disclosures

The account agreement and signature card disclose many of the terms and conditions of the account. In addition, the government requires credit unions to give members other disclosures designed to protect consumers and inform them about account practices. For example, if a member opens a share draft account, the credit union employee must provide a written disclosure on when funds from checks deposited to the account will be available to the member to use. Also, credit unions must provide information on dividend rates and fees in a uniform manner so that consumers can compare rates at different financial institutions.

Many credit unions combine these disclosures with other information in a member information packet that they distribute to all new members.

Member Identification Card

After joining the credit union, credit unions usually give members a member identification card (see figure 2.4 for a sample). This card helps the member keep a handy record of his or her primary account number and credit union locations, phone numbers, and web site address (if applicable).

Figure 2.4 Sample Member Identification Card

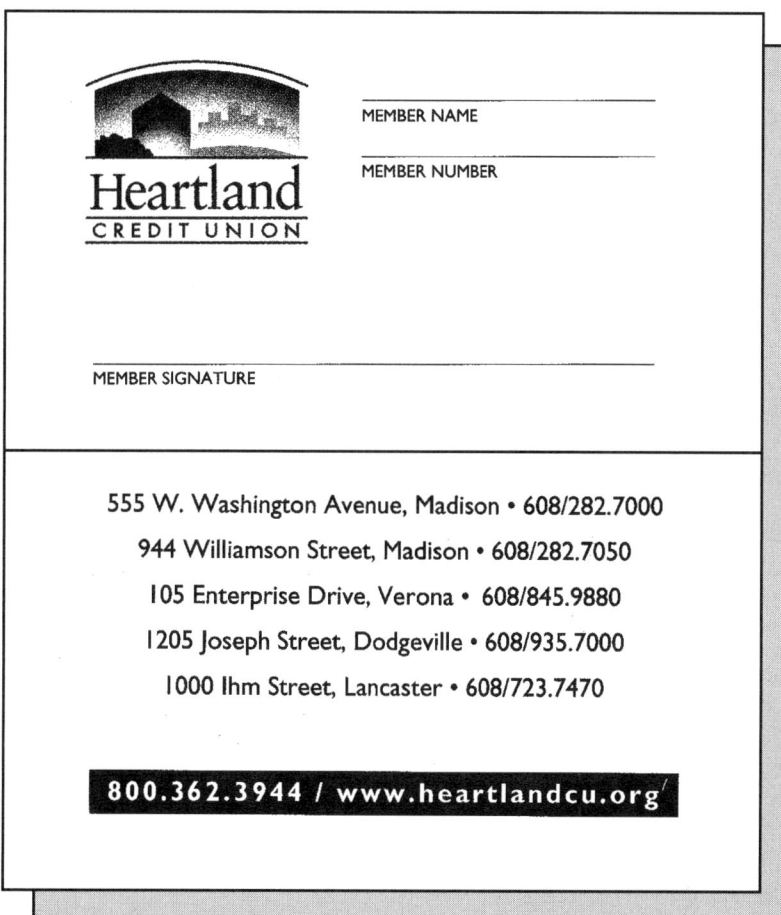

Source: © Heartland Credit Union, Madison, Wisconsin. Reprinted with permission.

To learn more about your credit union's account opening procedures, complete activity 2.2.

Member Services

OPENING AND ADMINISTERING MEMBERSHIP ACCOUNTS

Activity 2.2 What Are Your Credit Union's Account-Opening Procedures?

Obtain copies of the documents your credit union uses for new members to open accounts. Compare these documents to the ones shown in this chapter. How are the documents similar and how are they different?

_____
_____
_____
_____

Find out what the differences mean and if they are based on state law or credit union policy.

Closed and Dormant Accounts

Every credit union has different requirements and procedures for closing a member's primary (membership) account. Typically, as long as the member wishes to maintain other accounts or services with the credit union, the basic share account must remain open. Some credit unions relax this requirement if the member has an IRA or other type of savings account.

Inactive **(dormant)** accounts are also addressed in a variety of ways. Many credit unions send a notice to the member if the account has been dormant for a specified length of time. This notice serves as a reminder that the credit union appreciates the member's business and would like to have more of it. Occasionally, credit unions impose fees if a member's primary account remains inactive (meaning no deposits, withdrawals, or related activity) over a period of time. Usually, credit unions take action on these accounts only if the member is not using any other credit union accounts or services.

State laws require that credit unions turn over money in inactive accounts to the state government after a specified number of years. The credit union attempts to contact members before it turns over funds to the state. This is an important reason why members should keep their address records up-to-date at the credit union.

Decedent Accounts

When an account holder dies, the account, regardless of its ownership, becomes classified as a decedent account. (A **decedent** is another term for a deceased person.) A designated party or a legal representative of the decedent's estate may either withdraw or transfer funds in a decedent account to another account. Properly handling a decedent account is the final service that a credit union can do for the deceased member.

The credit union's responsibilities for decedent accounts begin when notified of the member's death. The major problem facing a credit union when handling decedent accounts involves making the funds available only to the proper parties. The account contract and state law determine the proper parties.

The ownership of the account is the most important factor affecting who receives the funds in the event of an owner's death. If the account is a joint tenancy with right of survivorship, the funds in the account belong to the surviving joint owner or owners. If the account has a designated beneficiary, then the credit union pays the account funds to that beneficiary.

Accounts in sole ownership require other procedures because the funds in this type of account are considered to be part of the deceased person's estate. Here is how this process works. A person dies either with or without a will. A **will** is a legal document that specifies how to dispose of a decedent's property (or **decedent's estate**) after death. A person who dies with a will is said to have died **testate**. A decedent without a will dies **intestate**. In either case, the state probate court oversees the proper distribution of the decedent's property. The court approves or appoints an individual to handle the estate. This person comes to the credit union with the proper documentation to obtain control of the account funds.

Services for Special Member Groups

Credit unions may develop special clubs or packages of services for certain groups of members. Examples are savings goal accounts, children's clubs, service packages for young people, and service packages or clubs for older members.

Savings Goal Accounts

Members often save money to achieve a particular financial goal. Credit unions may offer pre-designated accounts to help members save for these goals. For example, Christmas club accounts are targeted to members who want a separate account designated specifically for Christmas expenses. With these accounts, the member makes weekly or monthly deposits and the accounts are usually closed automatically in the fall with the funds being mailed to the member or transferred to another account. Members who use these accounts may receive a small gift, such as a Christmas ornament. The accounts usually earn rates comparable to regular share accounts. The account may require a small penalty for early withdrawal to give the member incentive to keep these funds in the account for the designated time period.

Member Services
OPENING AND ADMINISTERING MEMBERSHIP ACCOUNTS

In addition to Christmas clubs, some credit unions offer vacation club accounts or "dream" goal accounts where the member sets the particular goal. These accounts usually operate like Christmas club accounts.

Children's Clubs

Children who join credit unions learn good savings habits early, and can become the most valued members as adults. Credit unions realize the benefit of attracting more young people before they become customers of other financial institutions. Attracting young people into the credit union provides diversity and stability for the future. A children's club program is also a valuable benefit for members who are parents. These programs can assist parents in the financial education of their children while also providing an environment for fun.

Children's clubs are usually aimed at children under the age of thirteen and may include benefits such as low balance requirements on accounts, newsletters, calendars, birthday cards, savings banks, a special mascot, and scheduled events for children. Events can include art contests, summer picnics, holiday parties, and athletic events. Most services are free or at low cost to encourage children and parents to participate. Events for children can also serve as excellent community/member relations programs. (See figure 2.5 for a sample brochure on a children's club.)

Service Packages for Young People

Children "graduate" from children's clubs in their teen years; they need different services from the credit union. They may have income from jobs and begin managing their own money and expenses. ATM and debit cards may be part of a special service package for young people. Eventually, share draft accounts and education loans may respond to needs of these members.

Service Packages or Clubs for Older Members

The value of older members to your credit union has been well-documented. People over the age of fifty have higher savings balances, more disposable income, greater loyalty to their financial institution, and fewer account transactions than any other age group. They tend to be more concerned about the security of their funds, and they are more appreciative of personal service than are younger members. Today, this segment of our population is even more important due to the 76 million members of the baby boom generation. Credit unions need to position themselves against competitors seeking to serve this fast-growing group.

Children who join credit unions learn good savings habits early, and can become the most valued members as adults.

Member Services
OPENING AND ADMINISTERING MEMBERSHIP ACCOUNTS

Figure 2.5 Sample Brochure for Children's Club

What is the Super Savers Club?

The Super Savers Club is a savings account for children age 12 and under. Its primary purpose is to teach young people financial responsibility and money management in a fun and exciting way.

Who is the Great Dane?

Our Great Dane is the mascot for our Super Savers Club. He's a big purple dog who loves children and encourages them to save and spend their money wisely.

The Great Dane sponsors fun events throughout the year and all Super Savers may take advantage of them. Children will also receive periodic issues of "Pawprints," the Great Dane's newsletter that's written just for them!

Saving is FUN!

Each child who opens a Great Dane account will receive a Super Savers starter kit which includes a zippered money bag, savings account register, member ID card, a coin saver book, and other fun items.

Children can earn incentive prizes for deposits they make. We'll stamp their Great Dane Pawprint Stamp Book for every $10 they deposit. Along the way, we'll award them with prizes!

Parents can also help their children to save. It's easy through payroll deduction!

Dividends, too!

Children learn how their money will earn more money in the credit union than it will in their piggy bank because of dividends.

Dividends are paid quarterly on balances of $25 or more.

How to Join

Anyone living or working in Dane County is eligible to become a member of Dane County Credit Union. Plus, immediate family members may also join.

To join the Super Savers Club, all you'll need is you child's Social Security number and a minimum deposit of $25.

Start your child on the right track to saving habits that will last a lifetime! Open a Super Saver account today.

Source: © Dane County Credit Union, Madison, Wisconsin. Reprinted with permission.

OPENING AND ADMINISTERING MEMBERSHIP ACCOUNTS

Credit unions have found that accounts designed for the special interests of older members are effective in retaining existing members and attracting additional members within this age group. The services, events, and special features related to these accounts can also benefit members by providing them with additional financial services, conveniences, discounts, and social functions.

When designing a program for older members, credit unions often offer a package made up of several attractive elements. The following is a partial listing of the more common services included in these special accounts.

- **Membership in MEMBERS Prime Club.** This organization is a non profit corporation affiliated with CUNA Mutual Group, CUNA & Affiliates, and state credit union leagues. The club features a wide spectrum of discounts, savings and services providing extra value to members and their families. Examples include a subscription to a bi-monthly publication, accidental death and disability insurance, and discounts on hotel rates, vacation packages, prescriptions, vision products and services, and more. The program also includes assistance on retirement planning and management.

- **Special and reduced rate services at the credit union.** Credit unions frequently reduce or eliminate charges on programs such as share draft accounts and credit cards for their older members. In addition, credit unions offer services such as notary service, money orders, traveler's checks, use of copy machines, and wire transfers at little or no charge.

- **Access to consumer literature.** Many consumer newsletters and pamphlets of interest to older members are available through CUNA. Additionally, many credit unions supply leaflets from the IRS, Social Security Administration, and state insurance commission.

- **Retirement counseling and information.** Credit unions supply this service by using their own qualified staff members or by contracting with outside agencies or individuals.

- **Special savings programs.** A selection of high-yielding savings, investment, and IRA programs is of great importance in attracting and retaining older members.

- **Special meetings and events.** Many credit unions hold regular meetings and invite outside speakers to discuss such topics as retirement planning, travel, taxes, estate planning, and other areas of interest to older members. Credit unions can also organize field trips or special outings, such as trips to museums, performances, sporting events, and malls.

- **Directory of local discounts.** Many establishments offer senior citizen discounts. Credit unions may provide members with this information to help them save money. Some credit unions have even arranged special "members only" discounts with area businesses.

Just as your credit union needs to attract young members, it also needs to retain older ones. Programs for older members are an excellent way to benefit both the member and the credit union.

Complete activity 2.3 to learn more about your credit union's accounts and services for special member groups.

Activity 2.3 For What Special Member Groups Does Your Credit Union Provide Services?

What special accounts or services does your credit provide for the following groups:

Children

_____

Young People

_____

Older Members

_____

Other (if any)

_____

Chapter 3 Savings Accounts

One of the main reasons for founding the credit union movement was to provide members a place to save money and earn a good return. In this chapter you will review the general characteristics of savings accounts. You will also examine common types of savings accounts and how they differ in terms of access to the funds, rate of return, and other features. You will learn the primary benefits of these accounts so that you can best explain their use to members.

Characteristics of Savings Accounts

Why are credit union savings accounts called *share accounts?* Credit unions are cooperatives with a democratic structure. Members have an equal voice in the credit union because they own a "share" of the organization. Members are, therefore, doing more than just opening a savings account. When they deposit their funds, they become part owners of the credit union.

The different types of savings, or share, accounts have several aspects that generally apply to all types of accounts:

- dividends;
- minimum balance requirements;

Objectives

Upon completion of this chapter, you will be able to

1. **explain typical characteristics of savings accounts;**
2. **define *dividend rate, annual percentage yield (APY), daily balance,* and *average daily balance;***
3. **describe how compounding increases the yield of a savings account;**
4. **describe key features of life savings insurance;**
5. **list and explain the typical features and member benefits of regular savings (share) accounts, share certificates, and money market accounts;**
6. **differentiate among traditional IRAs, Roth IRAs, SEP IRAs, and Education IRAs.**

- account fees;
- transaction rules or restrictions;
- account statements;
- share insurance.

In addition, some credit unions offer life savings insurance on members' deposits.

Dividends

In general, credit unions pay dividends on deposits in savings accounts. **Dividends** are paid out of the earnings of a credit union and vary according to the financial

Member Services
SAVINGS ACCOUNTS

performance of a credit union. Credit unions pay dividends because the members' shares in the credit union are considered to be equity investments (a share of ownership) in the credit union. Just as stock in a corporation is considered to be ownership of the company and earns dividends for the stockholders, share savings accounts are considered ownership in the credit union and earn dividends for the members. (However, in some states, state-chartered credit unions are required to use terminology such as *interest* and *interest rate* rather than *dividend* and *dividend rate*. You may need to adjust your understanding of the terminology used in this chapter depending on the laws in your state.)

Simple Calculation of Dividends

Let's first look at calculation of dividends in a simple way. Three elements determine the calculation of dividends: principal, time, and dividend rate. The **principal** is the amount of money on which the dividend is to be calculated. For example, if you deposit $1,000 in your credit union, the original principal balance is $1,000.

Time refers to the period of time for which the dividend is to be calculated. Dividend rates are based on an annual period that is then divided into the payment period that applies to a particular account. Credit unions typically add dividends to accounts monthly, quarterly, semiannually, or annually (depending on the type of account).

Dividend rate refers to the annual percentage that will be applied to the principal to calculate the dividend. For example, assume a member has $100 in an account and the stated dividend rate is 6 percent per year.

$$\$100 \times 6\% = \$6.00$$

The member's dividend would be $6.00 for that year. Or, if an account earns an annual dividend of 4 percent, and the dividends are credited quarterly, then the account would earn one-fourth of the dividend (or 1 percent) in the quarter. This amount would be credited to the account and would show on account statements.

Calculating Account Balance

Another factor that affects dividend calculation is the method for determining the balance (or principal) on which dividends are calculated. For accounts that have transactions during a dividend period, the balance fluctuates and it becomes more complex to calculate a dividend. For example, assume an account earns monthly dividends and starts the month with a balance of $300. On the second day of the month, the member deposits $100. On the tenth day of the month, the member withdraws $50. On the twentieth day of the month, the member deposits $200. At the end of the month, how do you take these fluctuations into consideration and pay the dividend?

Under federal law, the credit union decides which of two rules it will follow for determining the balance: daily balance or average daily balance. With the **daily balance** method, the credit union applies a daily rate to the full amount of principal in the account each day. Usually, the daily rate is determined by dividing the annual dividend rate by 365, the number of days in the year (or 366 in a leap year). Each day the credit union's computer system multiplies the account balance by the daily dividend rate to determine that day's accrued dividend. (An accrued dividend is one that has been calculated but not yet credited to the account.) For example, if an account has an annual dividend rate of 3 percent and a balance of $100, the calculation for one day's accrued dividend would be

$$\frac{3\%}{365} \times \$100 = .82$$

At the end of the dividend period (usually monthly or quarterly), the total accrued dividends are credited to the account.

With the **average daily balance** method, the credit union applies a periodic rate (such as a monthly or quarterly rate) to the average daily balance in the account for the period. The average daily balance is determined by adding the full amount of principal in the account for each day of the period and dividing the figure by the number of days in the period. For example, on an account where the dividend is calculated monthly, the computer system would take each day's balance for the month, add them together, and divide by the number of days in the month. This result would be multiplied by the monthly dividend rate to determine the month's dividend.

Complete activity 3.1 to find out more information about dividends at your credit union.

Compounding

The Truth-in-Savings Act (TISA) requires credit unions to report the annual percentage yield on accounts to members. The **annual percentage yield (APY)** is a percentage rate that reflects the total amount of dividends paid on an account based on the dividend rate and the frequency of compounding for a 365-day period and calculated according to rules set out in the TISA.

When an account compounds, it means that when dividends are credited to the account, the dividends begin earning dividends. Consider the following example. An account pays a dividend rate of 3.44 percent. If the account did not compound dividends, a $10,000 balance in this account would earn $344 after one year ($10,000 x 3.44 percent). However, assume the dividends compound monthly and are credited to the account. The dividends are now considered to be part of the account balance when dividends are calculated for the next month. After a year, this monthly compounding results in an APY of 3.50 percent (compared to the dividend rate of 3.44 percent). With the monthly

---

When an account compounds, it means that when dividends are credited to the account, the dividends begin earning dividends.

Member Services

SAVINGS ACCOUNTS

Activity 3.1 How Are Dividends Calculated at Your Credit Union?

1. Why are earnings called *dividends?*

2. How is the account balance determined at your credit union (daily balance or average daily balance)?

3. When are dividends paid at your credit union? Is the payment the same for all accounts or different for some?

---

compounding, a $10,000 balance in this account would earn $350 after one year (if the dividends remain in the account for the year). (See figure 3.1 for an example of a rate chart reporting both dividend rates and annual percentage yields.)

The relationship between the dividend rate and APY varies depending on the frequency of compounding. More frequent compounding would increase the yield significantly. In general, the more frequent the compounding, the higher the yield.

Compounding dividends is an important concept to understand because it affects the yield paid to members on their savings. In today's highly competitive environment, earning the maximum yield is foremost in most members' financial planning.

See figure 3.2 for an example of a dividend compounding calculation.

Two simple rules illustrate the long-term effects of compounding. The first is the **Rule of 72.** You can roughly calculate the number of years it will take savings to double in value by dividing 72 by the annual percentage yield. Here's how it works: Suppose a member put $1,000 into an account at 4.5 APY. Divide 72 by 4.5. The answer is 16, which means that in 16 years, the $1,000 will grow into $2,000.

The **Rule of 116** is similar. It tells how long it takes money to triple. Thus, using the previous example, 116 is divided by 4.5. The $1,000 triples to $3,000 in 25.8 years.

Complete activity 3.2 to practice calculating long-term yields on accounts.

Member Services
SAVINGS ACCOUNTS

Figure 3.1 Sample Dividend Rate Sheet

Current Rates
SAVINGS

▶ DANE COUNTY CREDIT UNION ◀

November 14, 2000 THRU November 20, 2000

Type of Investment	Minimum Deposit	Term	Dividend Rate	Annual Percentage Yield	Check Plus 4 Dividend Rate	Check Plus 4 Annual Percentage Yield
New Horizon	$2,000.00	Open	3.55	3.61	N/A	N/A
	$10,000.00	Open	4.80	4.91	N/A	N/A
	$25,000.00	Open	5.00	5.12	N/A	N/A
Certificates	$500.00	3 Month	4.79	4.88	5.04	5.14
	$500.00	6 Month	5.30	5.41	5.55	5.67
	$500.00	12 Month	6.00	6.14	6.25	6.40
	$500.00	18 Month	6.10	6.24	6.35	6.50
	$500.00	24 Month	6.30	6.45	6.55	6.71
	$500.00	36 Month	6.30	6.45	6.55	6.71
	$500.00	48 Month	6.45	6.61	6.70	6.87
	$500.00	60 Month	6.45	6.61	6.70	6.87
Regular Savings	$100.00	Open	2.50	2.54	N/A	N/A
Bonus Checking	$1,000.00	Open	2.50	2.54	N/A	N/A
Holiday Club	$100.00	Open	2.75	2.78	N/A	N/A
IRA INVESTMENTS						
Open Passbook IRA	Open	Open	3.00	3.03	N/A	N/A
IRA Certificates	$500.00	12 Month	6.00	6.14	6.25	6.40
	$500.00	24 Month	6.30	6.45	6.55	6.71
	$500.00	36 Month	6.30	6.45	6.55	6.71
	$500.00	48 Month	6.45	6.61	6.70	6.87
	$500.00	60 Month	6.45	6.61	6.70	6.87

Bonus Rate: If your certificate is $25,000.00 or more, add 10 basis points to rate.

To qualify for Check Plus 4, you must have a Dane County Credit Union checking account and use 4 other qualifying services. Please ask for a list of qualifying services.

Dane
COUNTY CREDIT UNION

2160 Rimrock Road • Madison, WI 53713 • (608)256-5665 / 1-800-593-3228
www.danecountycu.org

Source: © Dane County Credit Union, Madison, Wisconsin. Reprinted with permission.

Member Services
SAVINGS ACCOUNTS

Figure 3.2 Sample of Dividend Compounding

Compounded amount on $1,500 for 3 years at 6 percent per year, compounded semiannually (equivalent to 3 percent earned each 6 months).

Initial deposit	$1,500.00
Dividend for 6 months, $1,500 at 3%	45.00
Amount at end of first 6 months = $1,500.00 + 45.00 = $1,545.00	
Dividend for 6 months, $1,545 at 3%	46.35
Amount at end of second 6 months = $1,545.00 + 46.35 = $1,591.35	
Dividend for 6 months, $1,591.35 at 3%	47.74
Amount at end of third 6 months = $1,591.35 + 47.74 = $1,639.09	
Dividend for 6 months, $1,639.09 at 3%	49.17
Amount at end of fourth 6 months = $1,639.09 + 49.17 = $1,688.26	
Dividend for 6 months, $1,688.26 at 3%	50.65
Amount at end of fifth 6 months = $1,688.26 + 50.65 = $1,738.91	
Dividend for 6 months, $1,738.91 at 3%	52.17
Compounded amount at end of 3 years = $1,738.91 + 52.17 =	$1,791.08

Minimum Balance Requirements

Credit union accounts often have a minimum balance requirement. For example, an account may have a minimum balance requirement to avoid service charges. Also, a minimum balance might be required to earn dividends. (See figure 3.1 for examples of minimum balance requirements.)

Minimum balances are usually established to discourage very small share balances, which are expensive for the credit union to maintain. In maintaining the account, the credit unions incurs expenses such as data processing, printing, and postage. The philosophy behind minimum balance requirements is not meant to punish members for having small balances, but to encourage increased savings participation with the credit union.

Account Fees

Credit unions charge fees for different purposes. The major function of fees is to make sure that the cost of services is spread

Activity 3.2 Calculating the Long-Term Effects of Compounding

1. Apply the Rule of 72 and calculate how long it would take for $2,000 to grow to $4,000 at an APY of 3 percent.

2. Apply the Rule of 116 and calculate how long it would take for $2,000 to grow to $6,000 at an APY of 3 percent.

Answers appear in appendix A.

---

fairly among members. For example, a member who uses one service heavily, such as money orders or check copies, pays for the use of this service directly. Otherwise, this cost would be spread among all members (who may not all use these services) by way of lower dividend rates. See figure 3.3 for an example of fees charged on share accounts.

Transaction Rules or Restrictions

Accounts may have limits on transactions. Some types of accounts allow almost unlimited transactions of any type. Other accounts restrict withdrawals or other types of transactions to a certain number per month. Still other accounts restrict withdrawals and charge members a fee or penalty if they make withdrawals before a certain date. The types of restrictions for different types of accounts are explained later in this chapter.

Account Statements

Credit unions send periodic account statements to members. Depending on the type of account and activity, credit unions may send the statements monthly, quarterly, or just annually. Account statements often list the transactions for the period, the current balance, and the annual percentage yield. Many credit unions take advantage of statement mailings to send members information on a variety of services available to them.

Share Insurance

Share insurance protects a member's share balance against loss if a credit union fails and government regulators liquidate it. Such insurance guarantees that credit union members don't lose all their savings if a credit union is closed. This insurance covers all types of share savings accounts.

Member Services

SAVINGS ACCOUNTS

Figure 3.3 Sample Rate and Fee Schedule

This Rate and Fee Schedule sets forth certain conditions, rates, fees and charges applicable to your savings and checking accounts at Rogue Federal Credit Union at this time. The Credit Union may offer other rates and fees or amend the rates and fees contained in this schedule from time to time. Each account holder agrees to the terms set forth in this Rate and Fee Schedule and acknowledges that it is a part of the Membership and Account Agreement.

Effective Date: March 1st, 2001 / Effective through: March 31st, 2001

Account Rates and Terms

	Annual Percentage Yield	Dividend Rate	Minimum Opening Balance	Minimum Balance to Avoid Fee	Minimum Balance to Earn Dividends	Dividends Compounded	Dividends Credited	Dividend Period
Savings	2.52%	2.5%	$25	—	$100	Quarterly	Quarterly	Quarterly
Kitty Club (age 12 and under)	2.52%	2.5%	$5	—	—			
Money Maker 0–$9,999	2.78%	2.75%	—	$2,000	—	Monthly	Monthly	Monthly
" $10,000–$24,999	3.40%	3.35%	—	$2,000	—			
" $25,000–$49,999	3.92%	3.85%	—	$2,000	—			
" $50,000	4.18%	4.10%	—	$2,000	—			
IRA Accumulation	2.53%	2.5%	$100	—	$100			
Regular Checking	—	—	—	$200	—	—	—	—
Super Draft Checking	1.51%	1.5%	—	$500	—	Quarterly	Quarterly	Quarterly

Account Service Fees

Membership Share $ 25.00
Membership Fee (except children 12 and under) $ 5.00

Checking Accounts

<u>Regular Checking</u>
Monthly Service Fee if $200 minimum balance maintained   No Fee
Monthly Service Fee if balance falls below $200 $ 5.00

<u>Super Draft Checking</u>
Monthly Service Fee (if $500 minimum balance maintained)   No Fee
Monthly Service Fee (if balance falls below $500) $ 7.00

<u>Other Fees</u>
NSF Return Item $ 15.00 ($90 daily maximum)
NSF Paid Item $ 20.00 per item
Overdraft Transfer From Savings $ 3.00
Stop Payments $ 15.00 per item or series
Copy of Check (each) $ 5.00
Manual Handling $ 15.00 ($90 daily maximum)
Printed Check   Prices may vary depending on style

Source: © Rogue Federal Credit Union, Medford, Oregon. Reprinted with permission.

Figure 3.3 Sample Rate and Fee Schedule (Continued)

<u>Money Maker Accounts</u>
Monthly Service Fee if $2,000 minimum balance maintained	No Fee
Monthly Service Fee if balance falls below $2000	$ 10.00
Returned Item	$ 15.00 for checks written over monthly maximum

Check Card/ATM (Automated Teller Machines)

ATM usage at RFCU or Co-Op owned ATM's	No Charge
ATM's not owned by RFCU or by Co-Op:	(first four transactions per month free, then)
	$ .75 each
Overdraft Transfer from Savings	$ 3.00
Insufficient Funds to Cover Transaction	$ 15.00
Card Reissue Prior to Expiration	$ 5.00
PIN Reissue	$ 2.00

Miscellaneous Fees

Account reconciliation (1 hour min.)	$ 15.00 per hour
Account research (1 hour min.)	$ 15.00 per hour
Statement copy fee	$ 2.00 per copy
Deposited item returned NSF	$ 3.00 per item
Uncollected deposited item	$ 15.00
Money Order	$ 2.00 each
Travelers Checks	$ 1.00 per $100
Travelers Checks (Checks for 2)	$ 1.50 per $100
Legal Process Fee (garnishment, tax levies)	$ 15.00
Inactive Account Fee (after 18 months & accounts under $100)	$ 5.00 per month
Copy of Credit Union Check	$ 5.00 each
Stop Payment of Corporate Check (where allowed)	$ 15.00
Corporate Check Withdrawals in Excess of 1 per day	$ 2.00
Account History Printout	$ 2.00

(Fees may be assessed for other services requested, such as Fax, long distance phone calls, wire transfers, IRA administration, photocopy, and courtesy check fees.)

Member Services
SAVINGS ACCOUNTS

The primary provider of share insurance is the National Credit Union Administration (NCUA), an agency of the federal government. The NCUA provides the coverage through the National Credit Union Share Insurance Fund (NCUSIF). The Federal Deposit Insurance Corporation, or FDIC, provides equivalent deposit insurance for banks and savings associations. See figure 3.4 for the NCUA logo that is displayed at all NCUA-insured credit unions.

All federally chartered credit unions must be insured by the NCUA. In addition, many states require their state-chartered credit unions to carry NCUA share insurance coverage. The other state-chartered credit unions not covered by federal share insurance are covered by private insurers operating under state laws.

The amount of share insurance coverage for each member is partly determined by the account balance and partly by the ownership of the member's accounts. The rules for coverage are complex enough that employees need further training to answer in-depth questions from members. See the STAR module, *S800 Opening New Accounts,* for more information on share insurance.

Life Savings Insurance

Some credit unions offer life savings insurance on members' deposits. CUNA Mutual Group pioneered this program, which encourages credit unions to grow and retain deposits.

Key features of this program include:

- Members are automatically insured when they deposit their savings into eligible share accounts.

- The credit union pays for the cost of the insurance.

- The insurance coverage usually matches the amount on deposit in the savings accounts, up to a specified limit. For example, if a qualified member has $2,000 on deposit in a life savings-insured account and the member dies, the insurance policy would match the amount in savings, paying out a matching $2,000.

- The member chooses the beneficiary to whom the benefit will be paid. You should note that the beneficiary for a member's life savings insurance does not need to be the same person as the beneficiary on a payable on death account. The member

Figure 3.4 NCUA Logo

Your savings federally insured to $100,000

NCUA

National Credit Union Administration,
a U.S. Government Agency

can designate different people as account beneficiaries and insurance beneficiaries.

- The insurance has two coverage plans. The decreasing term plan is one where the percentage of coverage decreases as the member ages, and usually terminates at age 70. The other plan bases the benefit on the age of the member when the deposit was made. This plan encourages long-term deposits and has traditionally been the most popular plan.

Life savings insurance should not be confused with share insurance. Share insurance is a government-mandated coverage and only takes effect if a credit union fails. Life savings insurance pays out when the member dies.

Types of Savings Accounts

Although credit unions differ in the features of their account offerings, they frequently offer savings accounts in the following categories:

- regular savings (share) accounts;
- share certificates;
- money market accounts;
- retirement accounts.

Regular Savings (Share) Accounts

These accounts are the basic savings plan of credit unions. Generally, a member opens a regular savings account by paying $5 to $25 into the account. This amount is considered the member's "share." A **share** is a set amount of money members deposit in a credit union to become members. Essentially, a member must maintain one share in the credit union and that share confers ownership rights on the member. An important ownership right is voting for the board of directors and other business matters at the annual meeting of the credit union members.

Dividends are paid on the account (although some credit unions may set a higher minimum balance for the balance to earn dividends). The rate of dividends is usually low compared to other accounts at the credit union.

The accounts usually have few transaction limitations with deposits and withdrawals allowed at any time and in any amount.

Members enjoy several benefits from these accounts. Members may find that the regular savings account is the place to start when establishing regular savings habits. These accounts are also a good place to keep emergency funds or funds a member is accumulating to open a higher-balance and higher-yielding account such as a share certificate.

Share Certificates

Share certificates require the member to keep their funds in the account for a specified period of time, called the term of the account. Share certificates may be withdrawn on the maturity date of the account. If the member wants to withdraw funds before the maturity date, the credit union usually assesses a penalty. Individual credit unions establish the calculation of an **early withdrawal penalty,** which usually involves forfeiting a sum equivalent to a certain amount of dividends.

For example, Carla's credit union assesses a three-month dividend penalty on early withdrawals from 12-month share certificates. However, Carla needs the money in her account and withdraws it four months into the term. Carla will lose three months' dividend on the amount she withdraws.

Share certificates usually require a higher minimum balance than regular share accounts and pay a higher rate. Usually, the longer the term of the account, the higher the rate.

The main benefit of a share certificate is the higher yield of the account. The member agrees to the term restrictions and higher minimum balance in return for these yields. Share certificates are good ways for members to save for long-term goals because then the restrictions on withdrawals are not important and the higher yield is a worthwhile compensation for the restrictions. Or, members may feel that rates from other types of investments will decline in the near term and the member wants to lock in the current rate in a certificate.

Most credit unions give members advance written notice of their certificates' approaching maturity date and any changes in the certificate. Often, the credit union may automatically renew the certificate unless the member instructs otherwise. Check your credit union's renewal policies.

See figure 3.5 for a sample of a share certificate document.

Money Market Accounts

Money market accounts are a hybrid of other types of accounts. They require high opening balances like certificates. They offer high rates comparable to certificates but the rates rise and fall with market conditions. Like regular share accounts, they do not require members to commit their funds for a specific period of time. They also allow deposits at any time.

In a money market account, an unlimited number of cash withdrawals, transfers, and payments to loan accounts are allowed in person, by mail, or at an ATM. Certain other transactions, however, are limited to six per month (or four-week statement cycle). These limited transactions are preauthorized, automatic transfers or share drafts to another account of the member or to a third party. Of these six transactions, a maximum of three share drafts can be written to third parties.

Money market accounts also frequently offer tiered rates on the accounts. A **tiered rate** means that the account earns one rate on a specified balance and a higher rate if the balance exceeds a set

---

The main benefit of a share certificate is the higher yield of the account.

Member Services
SAVINGS ACCOUNTS

Figure 3.5 Sample Share Certificate

SHARE CERTIFICATE
(CERTIFICATE OF DEPOSIT)

Heartland CREDIT UNION

ISSUE DATE

SS/TAX ID #   CD #   MEMBER #

This certifies that there has been deposited in an account at Heartland Credit Union the amount of
payable to the account holder(s) as set forth below upon maturity as herein defined. This Certificate is subject to the bylaws of this Credit Union and any law, regulation, or rule affecting the account.

ACCOUNT-HOLDER (S):   OR
                    PRIMARY MEMBER

1. **Maturity; Automatic Renewal.** The Initial Maturity Date of this _____ month Certificate shall be
   TERM

   This certificate will be automatically renewed for _____ months or the **same term** and amount at the close of business on the initial or any subsequent Maturity Date at the rate then offered by the Credit Union on Certificates of the same Term, unless: (a) withdrawn within a 10 day period after maturity, in which case no dividends will be paid after maturity, or (b) the Credit Union provides timely notice of different terms and conditions for renewal of this Certificate, or (c) the Credit Union provides timely notice that it elects not to renew this Certificate. Earnings in the account at the commencement of a renewal term shall be deemed merged with principal.

2. **Notice.** Notice of the options regarding renewal of this Certificate will be sent to the first-named Account-holder at least 20 days prior to the maturity date.

3. **Earnings.** Said account earns dividends at the annual rate of _____ %, compounded: _____ with an annual percentage yield (APY) of _____ %. Said dividends are computed on the basis of a 365 day year (366 days in a leap year). Certificates not renewed shall earn no dividends after the last effective maturity date. Dividends shall be paid _____ to the ☐ Certificate, ☐ Account-holder(s), ☐ Share Account no. _____ . If dividends are withdrawn, APY does not apply. The annual rate is fixed.

   The liability for dividends declared by the board of directors on Share Certificate and Share Savings accounts shall terminate without penalty to the Credit Union upon the Credit Union entering an involuntary dissolution procedure, or if the commissioner shall take possession of the Credit Union under s.186.29 of the Wisconsin Statutes. Upon dissolution, the commissioner shall determine the priority of payout of the various classifications of savings. Wis. Admin. Code CU60.06

4. **Penalty.** If this Certificate is surrendered for payment prior to the initial or any subsequent Maturity Date, the Account-holder(s) shall forfeit an amount equal to 180 days dividends on the amount withdrawn unless the account balance is drawn below the minimum balance of _____ , in which case the penalty shall be imposed on the entire account balance.

   Earnings accrued and paid to the Certificate during the current term may be withdrawn without penalty on the day dividends are paid to the certificate.

   Said penalty shall be computed at the nominal (simple) interest rate being paid on the account, and may result in forfeiture of principal. To the extent necessary to comply with these requirements, deductions shall be made from the amount withdrawn or the remaining account balance at the Credit Union's option. The penalty prescribed will not be imposed for a withdrawal following the death of the account-holder(s).

5. **Withdrawals, Transfers, and Pledges.** If said Account-holders names are conjoined by the word "OR", then any one of said Account-holders may authorize any withdrawal, transfer, or pledge of this account.

6. **Security Interest or Lien.** Account-holder(s) hereby grant(s) a security interest in this account to secure any obligation owed now or in the future to the Credit Union by any Account-holder(s), unless (a) this Certificate evidences an Individual Retirement Account or other tax-deferred retirement account, (b) the obligation is created by a consumer credit transaction under a credit card plan, or (c) the obligor's right of withdrawal arises only in a representative capacity.

7. **Ownership.** This account is NON-NEGOTIABLE and is NOT-TRANSFERABLE, except on the books of the Credit Union. Title is held as checked below:

   ☐ This Certificate is solely owned.
   ☐ This Certificate is jointly owned by the parties named heron. Upon the death of any of them, ownership passes to the survivor(s). This is not a marital account.
   ☐ This Certificate is a marital account.

8. **Other.** _____

Your savings federally insured to $100,000
NCUA
National Credit Union Administration,
a U.S. Government Agency

TCCU Effective: 01-01-96

CREDIT UNION AUTHORIZED SIGNATURE
X
PRIMARY MEMBER SIGNATURE

JOINT MEMBER SIGNATURE

Source: © Heartland Credit Union, Madison, Wisconsin. Reprinted with permission.

47

amount. For example, a credit union may offer one rate on a balance between $1,000 and $4,999.99. If the account has a balance of at least $5,000, the full balance earns a higher rate of interest.

Money market accounts appeal to members because of the high rates and more flexible requirements than certificates. Members may use these accounts to "park" funds that they do not need at the moment but will need within a few months. Members who think that rates will be rising soon may also prefer to keep funds in a money market account while waiting for longer-term certificate rates to rise. Then, they can lock in funds at a higher rate while earning a reasonably high rate in the meantime.

Practice matching members' needs to different types of savings accounts by completing activity 3.3.

Retirement Accounts

Many credit unions offer a variety of retirement accounts to members. In general, the different plans offer members a way to save for retirement while also enjoying tax advantages.

The most popular type of retirement plans are **individual retirement accounts (IRAs).** Over the years that IRA and other retirement plans have been authorized by the federal government, the options for individuals have expanded and become more complex. Today, a member needs to carefully review his or her options before deciding on which type of plan to open. In this section, we will review basic differences among these types of plans. (For more information on retirement accounts, see the STAR module, *S810 Individual Retirement Accounts.*)

Traditional IRA

The **traditional IRA** allows members to contribute part or all of their compensation (for example, wages and salary) to an account. The amount contributed is limited by law and may be deductible or nondeductible from federal income taxes for the tax year it is contributed. The amount of an individual's income limits the contributed amount that can be deferred from current income taxes. While the contributions remain in the account, the earnings are tax-deferred until they are taken out of the account. The account owner can make contributions to the account until age 70 $\frac{1}{2}$ if he or she is still earning compensation.

The account owner can begin taking distributions from the account as early as age 59 $\frac{1}{2}$ if he or she wishes. When the participant takes allowable distributions from the account, the earnings are taxable as current income and the contributions that were deducted from taxes are also now taxable. This tax deferral feature is attractive to individuals because many people pay taxes at a lower rate during retirement.

If distributions are taken before age 59 $\frac{1}{2}$, the account owner may be liable for current income taxes and a 10 percent tax penalty for early distribution. (Some exceptions are allowed. For

Member Services
SAVINGS ACCOUNTS

Activity 3.3 Matching Member Needs to Savings Accounts

1. A retired couple (she is 65, he is 66) comes into your credit union with $20,000 to deposit in an investment account. With Social Security benefits and a pension from his company, they are receiving an adequate monthly income. They are interested in receiving the highest rate of return possible on their investment. What type of account would fit their needs?

   _____

   Why?

   _____
   _____

2. A single person in his early twenties comes in with $500 he received recently for his birthday. He will be graduating from college in a year and plans to move away then. What type of account would fit his needs?

   _____

   Why?

   _____
   _____

3. A couple in their thirties, with two school-aged children, comes in. The woman has just inherited $10,000 from her grandmother and wishes to invest it. They talk about a vacation the family will be taking in three months, a new car they are interested in purchasing, and braces for one of the children. What type of investment would fit this family's needs?

   _____

   Why?

   _____
   _____

Suggested answers appear in appendix A.

example, penalty-free withdrawals are allowed for first-time home buyers, individuals who become disabled, and individuals who have qualified higher education expenses.)

Roth IRA

The Roth IRA was named for the member of congress who sponsored the legislation creating this plan. The **Roth IRA** allows individuals to make contributions that are not deductible from current income but that accumulate tax-free earnings. Distributions are therefore tax-free. These plans also have income limits for determining who is eligible to contribute and how much can be contributed. At age 59 ½, the account owner can withdraw funds without taxes or penalties as long as the account has been open for at least five tax years.

Although these accounts do not offer upfront tax savings to the participants, many individuals greatly value the fact that the earnings on the funds are accumulating tax-free rather than simply tax-deferred. For a member who has many years to retirement, a Roth IRA can actually produce higher tax savings.

Simplified Employee Pension (SEP) Plan

An employer uses a **Simplified Employee Pension (SEP)** plan to make contributions to employees' retirement accounts. Each participant owns an IRA that receives the contributions under the SEP program. The employer's retirement contributions are divided among the participants according to a formula. These contributions are deposited directly into the employee's IRA. The employer decides each year how much (if any) to contribute to the SEP program for that year. A SEP contribution becomes the employee's property when it is deposited into his or her account.

A SEP can be sponsored by a sole proprietorship, a partnership, a corporation, a nonprofit organization, or a government agency. It can serve a single participant or thousands of participants.

The contributions under a SEP program cannot exceed limits set by the IRS and are adjusted annually. The advantage of a SEP program is that an employee can still make a regular IRA contribution even though he or she may have received a SEP contribution from the employer for the tax year. The employer's contributions do not create taxable income for an employee until he or she takes the money out of the IRA. The employer's contributions are tax deductible for the employer.

Education IRA

The **Education IRA** is not actually a retirement account. It is an account a parent or other person establishes to save money to pay for the future qualified education expenses of another person (who is under the age of eighteen while the contributions are being made). To be eligible to contribute, the participants must not exceed income limits. The amount of the annual contribution is limited and is not tax deductible. However, earnings are tax-free and withdrawals are tax-free as long as the account owner uses them to pay for the designated party's education expenses. For individuals who are saving for a child's education, an Education IRA gives future tax savings they would not otherwise have.

Find out more about savings accounts at your credit union by completing activity 3.4.

Activity 3.4 What Types of Savings Accounts Does Your Credit Union Offer?

Investigate the types of savings accounts offered at your credit union and fill out the chart below.

Type of Account	Minimum Balance	Term (if applicable)	Annual Percentage Yield
Regular Share Account(s)			
Share Certificates			
Money Market Account(s)			
Individual Retirement Accounts (IRAs)			

Do the accounts reflect the text's explanations regarding typical balances and dividend rates?

Chapter 4 Share Draft Accounts

Share draft accounts are important to credit unions because they are the keystone service upon which you can build a strong financial relationship with members. These accounts enable members to conveniently withdraw funds from the credit union and to benefit from regular dividends at the same time.

Credit unions developed share draft accounts in the 1970s; they were the first dividend-paying check-type account. Prior to that time, checking accounts at financial institutions did not give customers a return on their deposited funds. After credit unions began offering share draft accounts, other financial institutions also introduced checking accounts that paid interest. Today, there are only minor differences between the share draft accounts offered at credit unions and the checking accounts offered at other financial institutions.

This chapter will discuss both the technical and service aspects of credit union share draft accounts.

How Share Draft Accounts Work

Share draft accounts were developed to assist the payment and exchange of money. A **share draft** is similar to a check and is a written order to a financial institution from the member/customer to pay a specified amount of money to another party upon demand. A share draft can be used as payment anywhere in the world. The system that controls this interexchange is complex but can be explained in simple terms. The following example illustrates the process called share draft or check clearing. (Also, see figure 4.1.)

John Smith goes grocery shopping at the Verigood Grocery Store. Instead of making his purchases in cash, John writes Verigood a share draft on his credit union share draft account.

Objectives

> **Upon completion of this chapter, you will be able to**
> 1. **define *share draft* and explain its purpose;**
> 2. **explain how the share draft processing system works;**
> 3. **list and describe typical characteristics of share draft accounts;**
> 4. **explain benefits of share draft truncation;**
> 5. **describe common types of share draft accounts and their benefits to members;**
> 6. **describe the usual fees on share draft accounts and why they are needed;**
> 7. **explain how share draft accounts benefit credit unions.**

Member Services

SHARE DRAFT ACCOUNTS

Figure 4.1 The Share Draft Clearing Process

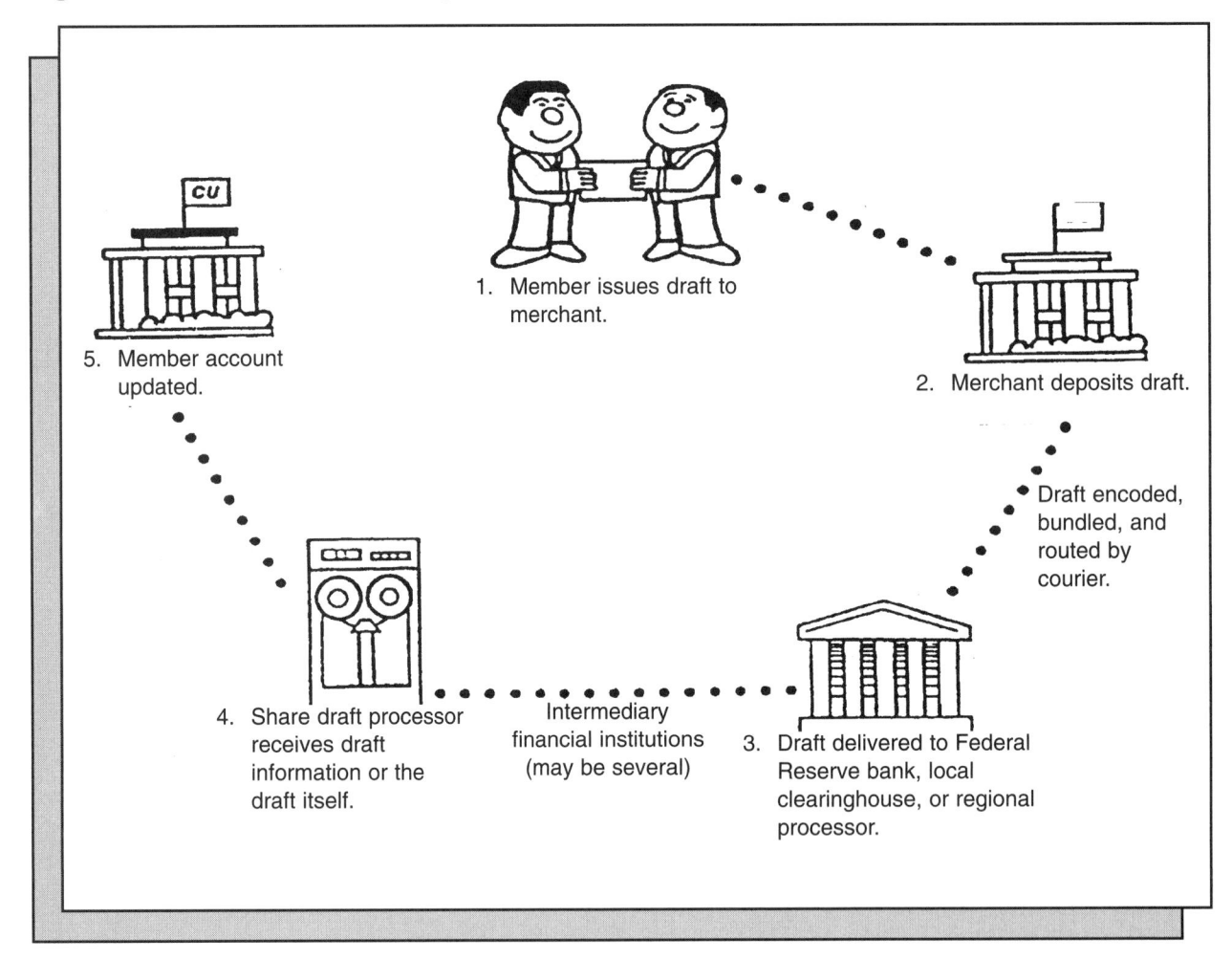

1. Member issues draft to merchant.
2. Merchant deposits draft.
3. Draft delivered to Federal Reserve bank, local clearinghouse, or regional processor.
4. Share draft processor receives draft information or the draft itself.
5. Member account updated.

Draft encoded, bundled, and routed by courier.

Intermediary financial institutions (may be several)

John's draft represents his promise to pay for the groceries.

At the end of the business day, Verigood deposits John's share draft into its bank account. Verigood's bank processes the drafts and returns it to John's credit union (or clearing bank). The amount of the draft is subtracted from John's account and credited to Verigood's bank, where it is added to Verigood's account. The transaction appears on the monthly itemized statement John receives from the credit union, so he can verify the purchase and balance his account.

Though some credit unions are directly involved in share draft clearing, some use other financial institutions' clearing systems. The illustration in figure 4.1 shows the role of these clearing systems in processing a share draft.

Complete activity 4.1 to find out about how your credit union's share drafts clear.

Member Services

SHARE DRAFT ACCOUNTS

Activity 4.1 How Do Share Drafts Clear?

Find out what method your credit union uses to clear its share drafts. Do they clear through a local bank? Out-of-town bank? Other method?

_____

_____

_____

_____

_____

How do all these share drafts get to where they're supposed to go? Obviously, if the financial institution issuing the draft and the one receiving it are in opposite parts of the country, the process can become involved. Before credit unions had share drafts, banks' checks were sorted and routed manually. By the 1950s, however, the volume of checks made automation necessary.

Today, computers accomplish the bulk of the check clearing process. Drafts and checks are sorted and identified through a series of numbers located along the bottom of the draft or check, known as the **MICR (Magnetic Ink Character Recognition) number.** The MICR number contains routing and transit information, and it identifies the financial institution and the Federal Reserve Bank district in which the draft (or check) was drawn. Figure 4.2 shows the circled MICR number. Specialists chose the properties of the ink used in the MICR number, as well as the shape of the specially designed numerals, to be universally acceptable to all computer sensors that decode the number. By reading and deciphering the MICR number, computers can identify, route, sort, forward, and pay the checks. Although the actual share draft travels from one spot to another, many of the debits and credits are processed electronically and faster than the transmission of the paper item itself. (A more detailed explanation and illustration of the check clearing process is described in the STAR module, *S100 Money and Negotiable Instruments.*)

55

Member Services

SHARE DRAFT ACCOUNTS

Figure 4.2 Sample Share Draft with MICR Number

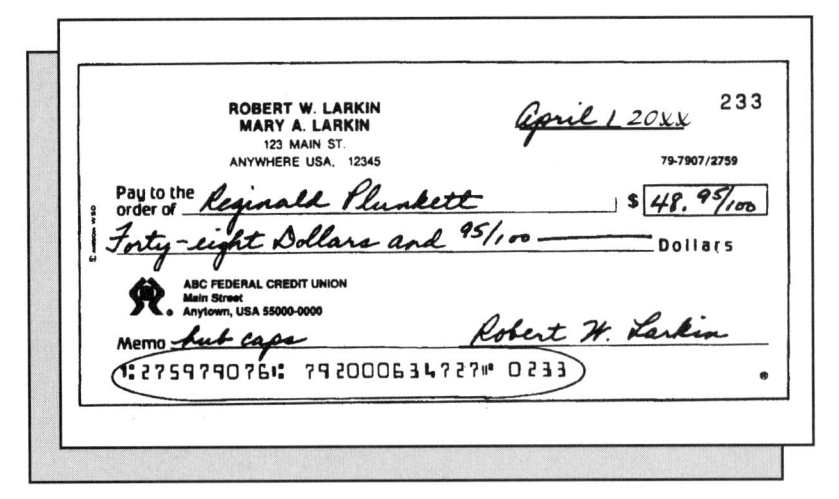

Characteristics of Credit Union Share Draft Accounts

Share draft accounts have a number of characteristics in common. Since they began offering share draft accounts, credit unions have usually offered the best bargain in town. They were among the first to pay dividends on checking-type accounts. In addition, credit unions also offer accounts that do not pay dividends but provide other benefits such as lower minimum balance requirements or account fees.

Since they began offering share draft accounts, credit unions have usually offered the best bargain in town.

Share Draft Agreement

Like other types of share accounts, members sign a share draft agreement when they open an account. The agreement covers the rules of the account such as how members should report errors on the account and how the credit union handles checks that would overdraw the account.

Monthly Statements

Credit unions send itemized monthly statements to members on the account (see figure 4.3). The statements list transactions such as deposits, dividend crediting, and cleared share drafts. Members use the statements to reconcile their records with the credit union's. Other types of accounts may also appear on the statement. Depending on the type of account, state and federal law may require other disclosures and terms. Check with your credit union management to understand what types of disclosures and terms are required for each account and how and when they should be given to your members.

Share Draft Truncation

Most credit union share draft accounts use **truncation,** which means the cancelled share drafts are not returned to the member with the statement. Instead, the member's share drafts are designed so that a duplicate copy is made each time a share draft is written. These duplicates can be compared later to the monthly statement.

56

Member Services

SHARE DRAFT ACCOUNTS

Figure 4.3 Sample Monthly Statement

Heartland CREDIT UNION

DIRECT INQUIRIES TO:
555 W WASHINGTON AVE
MADISON, WI 53703
www.heartlandcu.org
(608)282-7000
(800)362-3944

Member Name
Address
City/State/Zip

STATEMENT OF ACCOUNT

MEMBER NO.	ENDING DATE	BRANCH	PAGE	
0000000000	02-28-XX	1	1	13059 P

2519 — File your taxes online with Quicken and Heartland CU and get your return in 7–12 days! Go to heartlandcu.org and click on the Turbo Tax for the Web button. There's no software to download and you can stop and save at any time. Check it out today!

NOTICE: PLEASE SEE REVERSE SIDE FOR IMPORTANT INFORMATION

DATE	TRANSACTION DESCRIPTION	AMOUNT	FINANCE CHARGE	BALANCE
	REGULAR SHARE SAVINGS ACCT#1 02-01-01 THRU 02-28-01 PREVIOUS BALANCE			25.00
FEB28	NEW BALANCE			25.00
	HEARTLAND CHECKING ACCT# 2 02-01-01 THRU 02-28-01 PREVIOUS BALANCE			0.00
FEB01E	ADVANCE FOR DRAFT FROM/TO 142	1,217.51		1,217.51
FEB01E	SHARE DRAFT 1362 TRACE# 27392434	35.00–		1,182.51
FEB01E	SHARE DRAFT 1383 TRACE# 27403030	1,182.51–		0.00
FEB02	DEPOSIT 0202 1823 007733 555 W WASHINGTON AVE MADISON WI	532.23		532.23
FEB02	ADVANCE FOR CHECK FROM/TO 142	20.00		552.23
	0202 1824 007737 555 W WASHINGTON AVE MADISON WI			
FEB02	WITHDRAWAL 0202 1824 007737 555 W WASHINGTON AVE MADISON WI	120.00–		432.23
FEB05	DEPOSIT	171.89		604.12
FEB06	SHARE DRAFT 1396 TRACE# 77947024	12.00–		592.12
FEB06	SHARE DRAFT 1405 TRACE# 77866837	12.36–		579.76
FEB06	SHARE DRAFT 1404 TRACE# 77867164	12.65–		567.11
FEB06	SHARE DRAFT 1394 TRACE# 77886790	14.83–		552.28
FEB06	SHARE DRAFT 1395 TRACE# 77876111	16.91–		535.37
FEB06	SHARE DRAFT 1398 TRACE# 77891221	49.89–		485.48
FEB06	SHARE DRAFT 1399 TRACE# 77890589	55.11–		430.37
FEB07	WITHDRAWAL	77.17–		353.20
	POS 0207 0042 003549 OXYFRESH WORLDWIDE INC SPOKANE WA			
FEB07	SHARE DRAFT 1406 TRACE# 87092741	28.00–		325.20
FEB08	DEPOSIT	14.57		339.77
FEB08	SHARE DRAFT 1407 TRACE# 97215750	40.00–		299.77
FEB09	EFT DIRECT DEPOSIT/WIT CUNA INC PAYROLL 010209	1,019.00		1,318.77
FEB09	PAYMENT SHR TRANSFER 142Internet Access Feb. 08, 2001 21:10 Ref: 34180	1,210.00–		108.77
FEB09	WITHDRAWAL 0209 1825 007807 307 E WILSON ST MADISON WI	100.00–		8.77
FEB12	ADVANCE FOR DRAFT FROM/TO 142	8.08		16.85
FEB12	EFT DIRECT DEPOSIT/WIT LIBERTY CHECK CHK ORDER 020701	16.85–		0.00
FEB10E	ADVANCE FOR CHECK FROM/TO 142	108.77		108.77
	POS 0210 0201 008314 OXYFRESH WORLDWIDE INC SPOKANE WA			
FEB10E	WITHDRAWAL	108.77–		0.00
	POS 0210 0201 008314 OXYFRESH WORLDWIDE INC SPOKANE WA			
FEB12E	ADVANCE FOR DRAFT FROM/TO 142	156.18		156.18
FEB12E	SHARE DRAFT 1408 TRACE# 37428331	6.80–		149.38
FEB12E	SHARE DRAFT 1409 TRACE# 37437317	15.12–		134.26
FEB12E	SHARE DRAFT 1403 TRACE# 37455025	17.15–		117.11
FEB12E	SHARE DRAFT 1401 TRACE# 37475066	117.11–		0.00
FEB13E	ADVANCE FOR DRAFT FROM/TO 142	352.29		352.29
FEB13E	SHARE DRAFT 1414 TRACE# 47709963	8.62–		343.67
FEB13E	SHARE DRAFT 1410 TRACE# 47612002	12.12–		331.55
FEB13E	SHARE DRAFT 1412 TRACE# 47702373	56.25–		275.30
FEB13E	SHARE DRAFT 1402 TRACE# 47699972	62.30–		213.00
FEB13E	SHARE DRAFT 1413 TRACE# 47623271	100.00–		113.00
FEB13E	SHARE DRAFT 1411 TRACE# 47603738	113.00–		0.00
FEB13E	ADVANCE FOR CHECK FROM/TO 142	10.54		10.54

Source: © Heartland Credit Union, Madison, Wisconsin. Reprinted with permission.

57

SHARE DRAFT ACCOUNTS

Figure 4.3 Sample Monthly Statement (Continued)

NAME OR ADDRESS CHANGE

PLEASE CHECK YOUR NAME(S), ADDRESS, AND SOCIAL SECURITY NUMBER ON THE FRONT OF THIS STATEMENT. IF NOT EXACTLY CORRECT, COMPLETE THIS FORM AND RETURN IT TO THE CREDIT UNION OFFICE.

PLACE AN X IN THE FRONT OF THE ITEM(S) TO BE CHANGED

- ☐ Member's Name _____
- ☐ Joint Member's Name(s) _____
- ☐ Address _____
- ☐ City and State _____
- ☐ Signature _____
- ☐ Social Security No. _____
- ☐ Mail Code _____
- ☐ Telephone No. (___) ___ - ___
- Zip Code _____

PLEASE KEEP US INFORMED OF ADDRESS CHANGES

Each loan marked * is an open-end loan. The balance used to compute the FINANCE CHARGE on open-end loans is the daily unpaid principal balance. To get the daily unpaid principal balance, we take the beginning balance each day, add any new advances or debits, and subtract any payments or credits. The FINANCE CHARGE is computed by applying the appropriate daily periodic rate to the daily unpaid loan balance for the number of days the balance remains unpaid.

IN CASE OF ERRORS OR QUESTIONS ABOUT LOANS ON YOUR STATEMENT.

If you think your statement is wrong, or if you need more information about a transaction on your statement, write us on a separate sheet of paper at the address shown in the upper left corner on the reverse side of the statement as soon as possible. We must hear from you no later than 60 days after we sent you the FIRST statement on which the error or problem appeared. You can telephone us, but doing so will not preserve your rights.

In your letter, give us the following information:
- Your name and account number.
- The dollar amount of the suspected error.
- Describe the error and explain, if you can, why you believe there is an error. If you need more information, describe the item you are unsure about.

You do not have to pay any amount in question while we are investigating, but you are still obligated to pay the parts of your statement that are not in question. While we investigate your question, we cannot report you as delinquent or take any action to collect the amount you question.

IN CASE OF ERRORS OR QUESTIONS ABOUT YOUR ELECTRONIC FUND TRANSFERS (EFT)

Telephone us or write us at the phone number or address on the reverse side of this statement as soon as you can if you think your statement or automated teller machine receipt is wrong or if you need more information about a receipt or an EFT transfer on the statement. We must hear from you no later than 60 days after we sent you the FIRST statement on which the error or problem appeared.

1. Tell us your name and account number.
2. Describe the error or the transfer you are unsure about, and explain as clearly as you can why you believe there is an error or why you need more information.
3. Tell us the dollar amount of the suspected error.

We will investigate your complaint and will correct any error promptly. If we take more than 10 business days to do this, we will recredit your account for the amount you think is in error, so that you will have the use of the money during the time it takes us to complete our investigation.

CHECKS RECONCILIATION

OUTSTANDING CHECKS	
NUMBER	AMOUNT

ENDING BALANCE SHOWN ON THIS STATEMENT _____

PLUS DEPOSITS NOT SHOWN ON THIS STATEMENT _____

SUB-TOTAL _____

LESS TOTAL OUTSTANDING CHECKS _____

EQUALS ADJUSTED ENDING BALANCE _____

ADJUSTED ENDING BALANCE SHOWN ABOVE SHOULD AGREE WITH THE BALANCE SHOWN IN YOUR CHECK BOOK.

NOTE: BE SURE TO DEDUCT ANY CHARGES, FEES OR WITHDRAWALS SHOWN ON YOUR STATEMENT (BUT NOT IN YOUR CHECK BOOK) THAT MAY APPLY TO YOUR ACCOUNT. ALSO BE SURE TO ADD ANY DIVIDENDS OR ANY DEPOSITS SHOWN ON YOUR STATEMENT (BUT NOT IN YOUR CHECK BOOK) THAT APPLY TO YOUR ACCOUNT.

Recyclable Paper

Member Services

SHARE DRAFT ACCOUNTS

This truncated system is simpler and more convenient for the member for a number of reasons:

- It is impossible to forget to record a share draft because the duplicate copy remains in the account register.

- The account can actually be balanced from the duplicates, eliminating the need to keep a detailed check register. The member only needs to keep track of the account balance.

- The copies provide members with an instant reference source. These carbonless copies are also often accepted as proof of payment.

The credit union can store cancelled share drafts on microfilm or by using other electronic methods, relieving members of the necessity of storing bulky cancelled drafts. Copies can be provided to members, if needed, for a small fee or without charge.

In addition, some credit unions provide members with a small image copy of each cleared share draft (front and back) as a record of the check. These copies can be sufficient to prove payment when needed. Since the images are small and retrieved electronically, the credit union sends the copies along with the monthly statement. Members have the security of actually receiving a copy of the paid share draft and the credit union avoids the administrative cost of filing and returning share drafts to each member.

Complete activity 4.2 to find out more about truncation of share drafts at your credit union.

Activity 4.2 How Does Share Draft Truncation Work at Your Credit Union?

Find out about your credit union's systems and policies on share draft truncation.

1. How and where are your credit union's share drafts stored?

   _____

2. How does a member obtain a copy? What is the fee?

   _____

3. Does your credit union provide an image copy of cleared share drafts with statements?

   _____

Member Services
SHARE DRAFT ACCOUNTS

Types of Share Draft Accounts

As share draft accounts have evolved and grown in importance to credit unions, the credit unions have realized that different members have different needs that are not always met by a "one-size-fits-all" share draft account. Therefore, credit unions usually offer more than one type of share draft account. Following are examples of the types of accounts that are frequently offered:

- **Direct deposit of payroll and no dividends.** These types of accounts often have low or no minimum balance requirement. Also, the account may have low or no monthly account fees. The intent with these accounts is to offer an affordable account for the member who cannot keep more than a minimum amount in the account and is willing to accept no dividends in exchange for fewer requirements on the account. The requirement for payroll deposit usually means that the member will treat this account as his or her primary account for paying bills. If the credit union member keeps this type of account at the credit union, he or she is more likely to think of the credit union as his or her primary financial institution and the primary source of other financial services.

- **Direct deposit of payroll plus dividends.** These types of accounts often require a higher balance to avoid monthly service charges. The credit union needs to know that a set amount (such as $500 or $1,000) will always remain in the account before it can be financially feasible for the credit union to pay dividends on the account balance.

- **High balance accounts without direct deposit of payroll.** Again, credit unions are more likely to offer this type of account and pay dividends if the minimum balance requirement is sufficiently high to justify the dividends.

- **Accounts for special member groups.** As part of a package designed for special groups such as older members, college-age young people, or business owners, the credit union may offer an account that has incentives, such as low fees or balance requirements. For older members, the credit union may offer the account in combination with a requirement that the member have social security payments directly deposited to the account (which increases loyalty). For businesses, the credit union may offer an attractive share draft account in combination with providing other services such as employee retirement plans.

To design these programs, credit unions consider the makeup of their membership and which programs will appeal to members in ways that will encourage them to make the credit union their primary financial institution. (See figure 4.4 for examples of share draft account types.)

Figure 4.4 Sample Types of Share Draft Accounts

Heartland Credit Union   CHECKING ACCOUNTS: Effective Date 07/01/00

HEARTLAND CHECKING

Anyone who has electronic direct deposit of their net payroll check is eligible.
- No minimum balance or monthly service fee.
- No per check fee.
- TYME or HCU MasterMoney card with no monthly service fee is available to qualified members. *Transaction fees apply; see fee section.*
- No-annual-fee MasterCard is available to qualified members and if used at least 3 times per year.
- Overdraft protection is available to qualified members.
- Convenient duplicate checks.

REGULAR CHECKING

HCU's Regular checking is one of our most popular checking accounts. For a simple $4 monthly fee, you can write up to 30 checks per month.* There's no minimum balance requirement, and you receive convenient duplicate checks.
- TYME or HCU MasterMoney card is available to qualified members.
- Overdraft protection is available to qualified members

*First 30 checks per month—no charge. .25 cents per check written over 30.

MASTER CHECKING

Master Checking offers no-monthly-fee checking* while you earn dividends. Daily dividends are earned monthly and paid quarterly on balances of $2,000 or more. To open a Master Checking Account, simply keep a minimum balance of $1,000** in your Master Checking Account.

Master Checking also offers:
- TYME or HCU MasterMoney card with no monthly service fee is available to qualified members. *Transaction fees apply; see fee section.*
- No-annual-fee MasterCard is available to qualified members.
- Overdraft protection is available to qualified members.
- Convenient duplicate checks.

*First 50 checks per month—no charge. .25 cents per check written over 50.
**$10 monthly fee if balance falls below $1,000.

VARSITY CHECKING

HCU's Varsity checking is a checking account designed for students 21 and under. Student's parent(s) must be a member of HCU and Student ID or other verification is required.
- No minimum balance.
- No monthly service fee.
- Just .25 cents per check.
- TYME or HCU MasterMoney card is available to qualified members.
- Overdraft protection is available to qualified members.

PRIME TIMES CHECKING

HCU's Prime Times Checking, part of *The Prime Times Club,* is designed to meet the needs of members who are 50 years of age or better. Daily dividends are earned monthly and paid quarterly on balances of $2,000 or more.

To quality for Prime Times Checking simply:
- Have direct deposit of retirement, social security, or payroll checks, or
- Have at least $5,000 on aggregate deposit at HCU, or
- Pay $5.00 a month to be a member of the club.

Some of the benefits of the Prime Times Checking:
- Earn dividends.
- No-monthly-fee checking.*
- TYME or HCU MasterMoney card with no monthly fee is available to qualified members. *Transaction fees apply; see fee section.*
- No-annual-fee MasterCard is available to qualified members.
- No fee Traveler's Checks/No fee Cashier's Checks.
- Overdraft protection is available to qualified members.

*First 50 checks per month—no charge. .25 cents per check written over 50.

Bank-by-phone free of charge 24 hours a day with MARS, our Telephone Teller at 282-MARS or 1-800-362-MARS or online via our web site at www.heartlandcu.org

Heartland Credit Union is an Equal Housing Lender and savings at HeartlandCredit Union are federally insured to $100,000 by the National Credit Union Administration.

Source: © Heartland Credit Union, Madison, Wisconsin. Reprinted with permission.

Share Draft Services and Fees

As busy transaction accounts, share draft accounts have a greater variety of fees than most other share accounts. Examples include fees for share draft printing, monthly maintenance, stop payments, nonsufficient funds drafts, and statement balancing. (See figure 3.3 in the previous chapter for other examples.)

Although fees increase the cost of the account to the member, many surveys have shown that (on average) credit unions charge lower account fees than other financial institutions and members greatly appreciate this fact.

Share Draft Printing Fees

Obviously, the first fee charged is for printing the share drafts. The printing fee is usually deducted from the member's share draft account. In some cases, a credit union will provide the first fifty or 100 drafts free as an incentive for members to sign up for a new share draft account.

Monthly Service Charge

Credit unions may assess a monthly service charge on each share draft account. However, in many cases a member may avoid paying such service charges by maintaining a minimum balance in his or her share draft account at all times. For example, Credit Union A charges a monthly fee of $5 if the account at any time drops below $100 during the month. In contrast, Credit Union B charges a flat fee of $3 per share draft account, regardless of the amount of the member's balance.

Stop Payment Orders

A **stop payment order** is when a member authorizes the credit union to refuse payment on a share draft the member has written to another party. Members can authorize stop payment orders by telephone or in person. A signed stop payment order stays in effect for six months (unless renewed or canceled). Figure 4.5 is an example of a stop payment order.

Nonsufficient Funds

Occasionally, a share draft may be returned to the credit union marked NSF (nonsufficient funds). There may be several reasons for an NSF draft. A member may have made a mathematical error in his or her share draft register and simply may have written a share draft for an amount greater than the account balance. Or the member may have written the draft hoping enough money would be deposited in the account before the draft cleared. In any event, an NSF draft is expensive for the credit union because it means the draft has to be resubmitted and the funds collected.

Many surveys have shown that (on average) credit unions charge lower account fees than other financial institutions.

Figure 4.5 Sample Stop Payment Order

HEARTLAND CREDIT UNION
STOP PAYMENT ORDER

☐ ORAL REQUEST

SERVICE FEE WHICH WILL BE CHARGED TO DRAFT ACCOUNT

DATE OF DRAFT	DRAFT NUMBER	AMOUNT OF DRAFT	PAYABLE TO

DATE OF REQUEST _____

MEMBER NUMBER

MEMBER NAME AND ADDRESS:

Please stop payment on the draft described above, unless you have already paid, certified or accepted it. I understand that this request will take 24 hours before it goes into effect and will cease to be effective six months from the date shown below, unless previously cancelled or renewed in writing by me. The Credit Union will not be liable for payment of the draft contrary to this request unless payment is caused by the Credit Union's negligence and causes actual loss to me. The Credit Union's liability shall not, in any event, exceed the amount of the draft. I agree to reimburse the Credit Union for any loss it sustains in honoring this request.

_____
MEMBER'S SIGNATURE   Date

REASON FOR STOP _____   MEMBER'S PHONE NUMBER:

Source: © Heartland Credit Union, Madison, Wisconsin. Reprinted with permission.

NSF drafts may also be the first warning of fraud on an account. A member or another person may perpetrate the fraud. Your credit union management may have systems in place to alert the credit union employees quickly in these cases.

Balancing Statements

Your credit union may provide a share draft balancing service to its members. As its name suggests, the credit union balances the member's share draft statement for him or her. To some credit union members, balancing a monthly statement is confusing or difficult, and they welcome this added convenience. The cost of balancing a member's share draft account will usually vary from $10 to $25 an hour, depending upon the credit union's policies and available time to provide this type of service.

Overdraft Protection and Line of Credit

Many credit unions offer their members the convenience of a line of credit or overdraft protection, which is tied to the member's share draft account. The line of credit is preapproved, and the member can access it by writing a share draft. The interest rate is usually similar to that of a personal loan, and repayment is made on a monthly basis. (You

SHARE DRAFT ACCOUNTS

will read about the specifics of lines of credit in chapter 5.)

Tying this line of credit to a share draft account benefits the member by providing a cushion to avoid overdrafts. It is also a tremendously convenient way to access pre-approved credit. It is a strong selling point for your credit union's share draft account. Most credit unions do not charge for this service unless the member actually uses it. Many members seldom use the service but simply gain peace of mind from knowing that a share draft will not be returned if the member accidentally miscalculates the account balance.

Complete activity 4.3 to learn more about your credit union's share draft accounts and how they stack up against the competition.

How Share Draft Accounts Benefit Your Credit Union

Earlier in this chapter we stated that share draft accounts are a "keystone" service. In fact, for attracting and retaining some members, the share draft account is the most important service credit unions provide. A number of studies conducted by the Credit Union National Association/NFO WorldGroup and others identify some of the important benefits credit unions realize with share draft accounts. Let's briefly examine some of these findings.

- Checking and share draft accounts are critical financial services for consumers and therefore important services for attracting and retaining members. Of U.S. households, 90 percent have at least one checking account. Of credit union members, 96 percent have checking accounts.

- Share draft accounts are foundation services for developing a strong relationship with members. When members are surveyed about which financial institution is their primary financial institution, 72 percent name the institution that holds their most-used checking account.

- Researchers have found that the primary financial institution relationship is an important factor when members decide to obtain credit or other services. Members are more likely to first find out about needed financial services at their primary financial institution before shopping elsewhere.

- Members value the low fees of credit union share accounts, and loyalty is the credit union's reward. Of members who consider a credit union their primary financial institution, one survey found that 40 percent had free share draft

---

Share draft accounts are foundation services for developing a strong relationship with members.

Member Services

SHARE DRAFT ACCOUNTS

Activity 4.3 Comparing Share Draft Accounts

Obtain information about your credit union's share draft accounts and similar accounts at two competing financial institutions. Brochures are the handiest source. Phone calls to your competitors can also help you gather information. Then, fill out the chart below and see how the features of your credit union's share draft accounts compare to the competition. If your credit union and its competitors offer more than one type of share draft account, choose ones that are the most similar for comparison. Then, consider the benefits of your credit union's account and what features you would emphasize to interested members.

	Competing Financial Institutions		
	My Credit Union	Other	Other
Monthly maintenance fee			
Balance required to avoid monthly maintenance fee			
Cost for 200 printed share drafts/checks			
Number of free drafts/checks member can write per month			
Charge per draft/check in excess of free ones			
NSF fee			
Stop-payment fee			
Cost per copy of stored share draft/check			
Telephone inquiries			
Other features:			

65

SHARE DRAFT ACCOUNTS

accounts. In addition, of the primary members who paid a monthly fee, the average was $2.51. Non-members paid an average of $4.82 to their financial institutions.

Credit unions are successfully providing high value share draft accounts to members. Continued care and attention in this area pays off in the long run for the success of the credit union.

Chapter 5 Credit Union Lending

Credit unions were originally founded because working people could not borrow from other institutions at a reasonable rate of interest. Loans have long been identified as one of the major strengths of the credit union movement and an important reason many of your members initially joined your organization.

Credit unions make loans for almost any good purpose and have come a long way since the early credit union years. When credit unions were first established, they only offered personal loans. Walk into any credit union today, however, and you may find:

- signature (personal) loans and lines of credit;
- share draft overdraft protection;
- credit card accounts;
- education loans;
- business loans;
- several types of automobile loans (new and used);
- loans on other types of vehicles (such as boats, RVs, and motorcycles);
- home mortgage loans and home equity loans;
- loans against share accounts or stock;
- computer loans.

Objectives

Upon completion of this chapter, you will be able to
1. **differentiate open-end and closed-end credit;**
2. **describe how the creditworthiness of loan applicants is evaluated;**
3. **differentiate secured and unsecured loans;**
4. **explain how repayment risk and other factors affect loan rates;**
5. **describe typical features and benefits of credit insurance plans.**

Regardless of the department in which you work, chances are that at some time you be will asked a question about loans.

This chapter covers basic loan concepts that apply to most types of loans. (Chapter 6 covers types of loans.) Most loans and other types of credit can be categorized in several different ways. They also include many common features. This section lays down a foundation of knowledge about loans by explaining:

- open-end and closed-end credit;
- payment schedule;
- borrower creditworthiness;
- loan security—unsecured and secured loans;
- repayment risk and loan rates;
- credit insurance.

Open-End and Closed-End Credit

Loans and other types of credit are either open-end or closed-end. **Closed-end** is a general term used to describe a one-time extension of credit. With closed-end credit, each loan is handled as an individual and separate transaction with a definite term, or end date. A closed-end loan must be viewed as a single unit.

With a closed-end loan, the number of payments and the date of the loan's maturity can be calculated precisely. If the member makes all payments as scheduled, the loan is paid off at maturity. An example is a 48-month automobile loan.

Closed-end loans can have substantial paperwork and are often made for sizable sums of money, such as what is needed to purchase an automobile or home. The federal government also requires more complex disclosures of finance charges on closed-end loans.

Under an **open-end** credit plan, the member makes a one-time application to obtain credit for use on an ongoing or revolving basis. Open-end credit is extended to the member under a plan that meets three conditions:

1. The member can obtain credit from time to time, either directly from the credit union, or indirectly by the use of a credit card or other device.
2. The credit limit is set by the credit union and that amount is made available, minus any outstanding balance. For example, if the credit limit is $1,000 and the member has $300 outstanding, then the member can access $700 of additional funds.
3. The credit union may compute a finance charge (usually monthly) on the outstanding unpaid balance.

Open-end loans have less paperwork and disclosures of finance charges are simpler. For a member who repeatedly needs to borrow funds, open-end credit makes the process faster and less complicated.

Payment Schedule

Several payment schedules are used with loans and other credit. The most common type of payment schedule is set up on a monthly basis. Some loans require only one payment at the end of the loan term. This type of schedule may be used for a short-term loan. Although rare at credit unions, another type of payment is a balloon payment. With this type, the member makes regular monthly installments (of either interest only or interest and a small portion of the principal) and then makes a large final payment at the end of the term.

Sometimes unforeseen events, such as sickness, accident, or layoff, make it impossible for a member to meet loan obligations. In these cases, the member may request a payment extension (a

---

Open-end loans have less paperwork and disclosures of finance charges are simpler.

delay of one or more payments). If the member has made loan payments long enough to considerably reduce the principal, the credit union may extend the loan (spread the payments over a longer term), lowering the member's remaining payments.

An advantage members have when borrowing from the credit union is the ability to prepay the loan without penalty. Credit unions compute loans on a simple interest basis, meaning members pay interest on the borrowed funds only for the time they use them. For example, a member receives a closed-end personal loan from your credit union, and payments are set up so the loan is paid off in twelve months. The member subsequently receives a large income tax refund and repays the loan in only eight months. The member saves four months' interest.

Borrower Creditworthiness

The process of evaluating the loan application is called underwriting, or determining the member's creditworthiness. Before a credit union grants any type of loan to a member, it evaluates the information on the member's loan application (see figure 5.1) and credit report on the basis of three factors:

- character, or the willingness to pay;
- capacity, or the ability to pay;
- collateral, or something of tangible value that can secure the loan.

Character, or willingness to pay, is the most important factor in determining creditworthiness. Credit unions differ from other financial institutions in the emphasis they place on character. This is due to their overall philosophy of promoting thrift and the wise use of credit and of extending service to all who need and can use it.

To evaluate a member's character, the credit union looks at evidence of stability and the credit report. Several indicators that show stability are length of current and previous residency, length of current and previous employment, proximity of personal references, and the credit union's past experience with the member.

The credit report is an important indicator of character. It shows the member's credit history in the following ways:

1. **Amount repaid.** This is the difference between the member's original balances and current balances on any loans he or she may have. The higher the amount the member has repaid, the better the indication that the debt will be handled responsibly.

2. **Amount of past credit compared to age.** The older the member the more credit history he or she is likely to have. For a very young member, lack of credit history

---

Character, or willingness to pay, is the most important factor in determining creditworthiness.

Figure 5.1 Sample Loan Application

Dane County Credit Union

LOAN APPLICATION

☐ **Individual Credit** - Complete the applicant section. If you are married and a Wisconsin resident, also complete the spouse section.
☐ **Joint with Spouse** - Complete both applicant and spouse sections.
☐ **Joint Credit** - If other applicant is not your spouse, you must complete separate applications, including the spouse sections if you are married and a Wisconsin resident.

Insurance Coverage Desired:
☐ I want disability protection for myself
☐ I want credit life protection for myself
☐ I want joint disability protection with co-applicant
☐ I want joint life protection with co-applicant

No provision of a marital property agreement, a unilateral statement under Wis. Stat. Sec. 766.59 or a court decree under Wis. Stat. Sec. 766.70 adversely affects the interests of the credit union unless prior to the time the credit is extended, the credit union is furnished with a copy of the agreement, statement or decree, or has actual knowledge of the adverse provision when the obligation to the credit union is incurred.

Amount of Loan $ | Purpose of Loan: | Date:

APPLICANT INFORMATION

Marital Status (Check one) ☐ Married year________ ☐ Unmarried ☐ Legally separated by court order
Name (First, middle, last) | Account Number
Full Address | How Long?
Previous Address (If less than 2 years at present address) | How Long?
Social Security # | Birthdate | Home Phone
Employer | Position | How Long?
Employer Phone | My Take-Home Pay (Net) $ | Per
Previous Employer (If less than 2 years at present employer) | How Long?
Applicant or Spouse Other Income*: Source | Net Monthly Amount $ | Ages of Dependents:
*Note: You need not list income from alimony, child support, or separate maintenance unless you wish it considered for purposes of repaying this debt.

SPOUSE INFORMATION

Name (First, Middle, Last) | Birthdate | Social Security #
Address and Phone (If different than applicant)
Employer | Position | How Long?
Employer Phone | My Take-Home Pay (Net) $ | Per
Previous Employer (If less than 2 years at present employer) | How Long?

CREDIT HISTORY

Year/Make of Auto | Financed By | Amount Owed $ | Rate | % Payment $
Year/Make of Auto | Financed By | Amount Owed $ | Rate | % Payment $
Mortgage Holder: | Home Value $ | Amount Owed $ | Rate | % Payment $
Other Assets: (Boats, other real estate, savings/retirement accounts)
Rent: Landlord Name/Phone | Payment $
List below all obligations including banks, finance companies, credit unions, and credit cards. Attach separate sheet if necessary.
Creditor: | Amount Owed $ | Rate | % Payment $
Creditor: | Amount Owed $ | Rate | % Payment $
Creditor: | Amount Owed $ | Rate | % Payment $
Creditor: | Amount Owed $ | Rate | % Payment $
Creditor: | Amount Owed $ | Rate | % Payment $
Cosigned for: | Amount Owed $ | Rate | % Payment $
Alimony, child support or maintenance paid to: | Obligation Ends: | Payment $
Is applicant or spouse a party in any legal action? ☐ yes ☐ no If yes, describe: | Bankruptcy?/Year:
Name, address, phone of relative not living with you:
Name, address, phone of friend / personal reference:

The undersigned certify that the foregoing information has been supplied truthfully, accurately and voluntarily, and therefore authorize this credit union to investigate our creditworthiness, credit history and financial responsibility through any credit bureau or by any other reasonable means. If this application is for the purpose of encumbering real property, the undersigned agrees to pay all allowable expenses incurred in processing this application whether or not the loan is approved. This application does not constitute a contract for the extension of credit. The undersigned understands that it may be a federal crime punishable by fine or imprisonment or both to knowingly make any false statements concerning any of the above facts, as applicable under the provision of Title 18, United States Code, Section 1014.

Applicant's Signature | Date
Spouse's Signature (if joint applicant) | Date

COMPLETE THIS SECTION ONLY IF YOU ARE MARRIED AND YOU ARE APPLYING FOR INDIVIDUAL CREDIT

I certify that the credit being applied for, if granted, will be incurred or obtained during marriage and will be in the interest of the marriage or family. This statement is made in accordance with Wis. Stat. Sec. 766.55(1). If this section applies, we are required by Wisconsin law to notify your spouse by mail if your loan is granted.

Applicant's Signature | Date

Dane County Credit Union, 2160 Rimrock Road, Madison, WI 53713
Phone: (608) 256-5665 Fax: (608) 284-4700

Source: © Dane County Credit Union, Madison, Wisconsin. Reprinted with permission.

is not necessarily negative. However, for a more mature member, a credit history usually contains significant information.

3. **Pattern of repayment.** Typically, credit reports will indicate the member's payment history on loans and other credit. Problems such as slow pay, repossessions, and collections are included. Also, bankruptcy filings are listed.

4. **Credit score.** Credit scoring is a system that uses mathematical formulas, also called scorecards, to determine the probability that members will repay loans. The system assigns point values (plus or minus) to different elements of a member's credit record. In general, the higher the credit score, the more likely the member will repay a loan.

Finally, the credit report gives basic information about the member, such as address, place of employment, and Social Security number. This information can be checked against the application for discrepancies.

The second factor used to determine creditworthiness is **capacity,** or ability to pay. Regardless of how solid the member's character may be, the member must be able to pay the debt.

To find the member's capacity, a **debt-to-income ratio** is calculated. This is done by dividing the member's total monthly income into his or her total monthly debt payments (including the payment on the loan for which he or she is applying, but not including monthly housing payment). Therefore, the calculation would be:

$$\text{debt-to-income ratio} = \frac{\text{total monthly debt payments (not including housing)}}{\text{total monthly income}}$$

If the ratio exceeds 25 to 30 percent, it indicates the member would probably have difficulty in paying any additional debts.

A second ratio, **total obligations-to-income,** may be calculated. This ratio includes the member's housing payment in the total monthly debt payments. This ratio should not exceed 40 to 50 percent, depending on the credit union's standards.

To develop your understanding of loan ratios, complete activity 5.1.

Debt-to-income ratios are a more accurate predictor of a member's ability to repay than simply the income itself. No matter what salary the member makes, it is the amount of money he or she has available after paying monthly debts that counts.

The third factor used to determine creditworthiness is **collateral**—something of value pledged to secure the loan. Whether or not a member can provide some collateral to secure a loan may decide the fate of that loan. Collateral is explained more fully in chapter 6.

Unsecured and Secured Loans

Although there are many different types of loans, all loans can be categorized in one of two

Member Services
CREDIT UNION LENDING

Activity 5.1 Calculating Ratios

1. A member who is applying for a personal loan has a monthly income of $2,000 and monthly debts of $500. What is the debt-to-income ratio?

2. This same member has a monthly housing payment of $400. What is the total-obligations-to-income ratio?

Answers appear in Appendix A.

---

ways: unsecured or secured. An **unsecured loan** is one made solely on the strength of the member's personal creditworthiness. No collateral is required. These loans are commonly called **signature loans** because the only guarantee the member gives promising to repay the loan is his or her signature. Unsecured loans can be made under a variety of different terms and for many purposes, which will be discussed in the next chapter.

A **secured loan** has collateral provided. Collateral on a loan provides something of value that can be sold or kept by the credit union in the event the member defaults on the loan. One of the most familiar examples of a secured loan is an auto loan, where the car serves as security for the loan repayment.

Credit unions may request that members provide security on their loans if they have little credit history, if they have had repayment problems in the past, or if their financial situation is unstable. However, just because collateral is required on a member's loan does not necessarily mean that the member could not qualify for a signature loan. Often, collateral is necessary because the amount requested by the member exceeds the credit union's signature loan limit.

Repayment Risk and Loan Rates

Interest is the return paid to those who lend money to firms or others. Specifically, interest rates are the prices paid for borrowing money for a period of time. This means that if the interest rate on a $1,000 loan is 10 percent per year, the borrower would pay $100 of interest for one year. If members borrow money from the credit union, they pay interest to the credit union as the cost of the loan.

Loan rates and terms are set by your credit union using several factors:

- repayment risk;
- competition;
- loan volume;
- fixed vs. variable rates.

Repayment Risk

The first factor is risk. When the credit union makes a loan, what is the risk of the member not repaying the loan?

Obviously, the highest risk loans are those made without any type of collateral. Thus, as you will notice in figure 5.2, the highest loan rate is charged for a signature loan. Credit card loans also usually have high rates compared to other loans.

Signature loans have more risk than other loans because no collateral is taken. If the member defaults on the loan, the credit union would have no claim on any of the member's possessions. Consequently, the credit union would have greater difficulty in collecting the loan.

Automobile loans, on the other hand, represent a lower level of risk for the credit union. If the member defaults on the loan, the credit union can repossess the automobile and sell the vehicle to recover some of its money. Thus, the loan rate is lower on automobiles because the overall risk is lower.

The lowest rates are usually charged on 100 percent share or share-certificate secured loans. In this case, the risk is very low because the member is essentially borrowing money that the member already has, and agrees not to withdraw it from the credit union until the loan is repaid.

Other factors affect the repayment risk. The term of the loan influences the risk, along with the nature of the personal property involved. For example, the highest automobile loan rates accompany a sixty-month loan (five years). As an automobile ages, its value decreases. Naturally, the member is eager to make loan payments on a new car because the member does not want to lose the car. However, as the car ages and other expenses arise, the member may be less willing to make those loan payments. Loan rates on long-term car loans are set at a higher rate to compensate for the higher delinquency rate experienced on longer loans. This is also the reason why rates on loans for used automobiles are typically higher than loan rates on new cars. Many credit unions may not have a used car rate for vehicles that are older than five or six model years.

Risk is also affected by the size of the down payment on certain types of loans. Large down payments on a consumer item (such as an automobile) reduce risk to the credit union. The more money a member puts down on the new vehicle, the less needs to be financed. The chance of default lessens because the loan can be paid off faster and the member has more invested in the vehicle that would be lost in the event of default.

Figure 5.2 Sample Loan Rates

LANCO Federal Credit Union
Loan Rates

Special Auto Rates

Term	Year of Vehicle	Rate
2–4 Year	2001	8.20% A.P.R.
5 Year	2001	8.50% A.P.R.
6 Year	2001	8.75% A.P.R.

New and Used* Autos

Term	Year of Vehicle	Rate
2.5 Year	1993–94	8.50% A.P.R.
3 Year	1995	8.50% A.P.R.
3.5 Year	1996	8.75% A.P.R.
4 Year	1997	8.75% A.P.R.
5 Year	1998–2000	9.00% A.P.R.

*The car must be a 1993 or newer.

Lease Alternative

Term	Year of Vehicle	Rate
2 Year	1996	9.00% A.P.R.
3 Year	1997	9.00% A.P.R.
4 Year	1998	9.25% A.P.R.
5 Year	1999	9.50% A.P.R.
6 Year	2000–2001	10.25% A.P.R.

Signature Loans

Type	Rate	Comment
Advantage Plus Line-of-Credit	12.49% A.P.R.	Variable rate $7,500 Maximum
Closed-End	13.50% A.P.R.	$7,500 Maximum

Sidebar navigation:
- Home Page
- e-Services
- Kids
- Who we are
- Loans
  - Loans
  - Loan Rates
  - Loan Calculator
  - Loan Application
  - LANCO VISA
  - Home Loans
- Savings & more
- Cool Stuff
- Site Map
- Newsletter
- Contact Us
- Special Events

Source: © LANCO Federal Credit Union, Lancaster, Pennsylvania. Reprinted with permission.

Figure 5.2 Sample Loan Rates (Continued)

Boat Loans

Term	Rate
3 Year	8.75% A.P.R.
5 Year	9.75% A.P.R.
8 Year	10.25% A.P.R.
12 Year	10.75% A.P.R.

Share Secured

Loan Amount	Rate
Equal to share pledge	7.50% A.P.R.

Home Equity Line-of-Credit

Loan Limit	Current Rate	Comment
Up to 80% of Appraisal (less existing lien)	9.75% A.P.R.	Variable Rate Loan $50,000 Maximum Line
81% to 100% of Appraisal (less existing lien)	11.75% A.P.R.	Variable Rate Loan $50,000 Maximum Line

Fixed Rate Home Equity Loans

Term	Current Rate	Comment
3 Year	7.90% A.P.R.	Call for additional info.
5 Year	8.75% A.P.R.	Call for additional info.
8 Year	10.00% A.P.R.	Call for additional info.
12 Year	11.00% A.P.R.	Call for additional info.

Mortgage Loans

Call For Quote and Other Information

Notes:
- A.P.R. means Annual Percentage Rate.
- All loans are subject to credit approval.
- Rates are subject to change at any time.
- When applying for a loan, LANCO Federal Credit Union will determine the interest rate based on credit history, work history, net income and current debt. Individual rates may be higher than the advertised rates. We will offer the best possible rate based on your qualifications.

| Who We Are | Loans | Savings & Checking | Cool Stuff | Kids Stuff | Contact Us |

© LANCO Federal Credit Union
Lancaster, Pa.
lanco@lancofcu.com

EQUAL HOUSING LENDER

Competition

A second factor affecting your credit union's loan rates is competition. Your credit union may lower its loan rates on new cars to match rates offered by a bank or other financial institution in your area. A credit union may have a money sale in which it offers reduced loan rates for a short period of time in response to the competition's promotional effort.

Loan Volume

A third factor affecting loan rates is the credit union's desire to promote certain types of loans. The credit union may lower its loan rates if it wants to make more computer or home equity loans. If loan volume is slow and the credit union wants more loans, nothing is more effective than lowering loan rates. On the other hand, the credit union may raise its loan rates if it wants to decrease loan volume. This situation may occur if the credit union does not have excess liquidity (funds) to make loans.

Fixed vs. Variable Loan Rates

Together, the factors of risk, meeting the competition, and the desire to promote loans affect loan terms and interest rates offered by your credit union. In addition, the rates are affected by whether the rate is fixed or variable. Some types of loans have a rate of interest that is **fixed** for the term of the loan. This is typical for auto loans.

Other types of loans may have variable rates. **Variable rate** means the interest rate on the loan will move up or down, depending on current market rates. Credit unions use variable-rate programs to better match the rates they are earning on loans with the rates they must pay on savings accounts.

Interest on variable-rate loans can be adjusted at set intervals, which can be as frequent as every month or at longer time intervals such as each year. A typical variable loan contract would specify the limits under which the interest rate could be adjusted. Sometimes, a cap of 2 to 5 percentage points increase is placed on the interest rate. This cap can apply to changes over a twelve-month period, or for the life of the loan.

Variable-rate loans offer both the risks and benefits of market rate changes to borrowing members. Members receive the lowest loan rates possible at the time, without having to rewrite their current loans.

Complete activity 5.2 to relate your credit union's loan rates to repayment risk.

Credit Insurance

Many credit unions also offer credit insurance to members who obtain loans. CUNA Mutual Insurance Society, the major provider of this type of insurance to credit unions, offers three types of credit insurance:

- loan protection insurance;
- credit life insurance;
- credit disability insurance.

Activity 5.2 Relating Loan Rates to Repayment Risk

Obtain a copy of your credit union's loan rate list and compare the rates to the previous discussion of repayment risk.

1. How much difference is there in rates for unsecured and secured loans?

   _____

   _____

2. Which types of unsecured loans have the highest rates? Why do you think this is so?

   _____

   _____

3. Which secured loans have the highest rates? Why do you think this is so?

   _____

   _____

Loan Protection Insurance

Loan protection insurance is provided by credit unions at no direct cost to members and reduces or pays off insured loan balances when members die. Coverage in case of total and permanent disability may be available. Joint life coverage may also be provided.

Loan protection insurance has benefits for credit unions and members. For a credit union, it differentiates the credit union's loans from other lenders that do not offer this coverage. It reinforces a credit union's image as a financial institution that's for people, not profit. It also benefits the credit union by reducing collection costs and charged-off loans that might be unpaid due to a member's death. Members benefit because they have "peace of mind" and reduction of the burden of a loan on survivors.

Credit Life Insurance

Most credit unions prefer to offer **credit life insurance** to members on a voluntary, member-pay basis. Under this coverage, the member's loan is reduced or paid off if they die before the loan is repaid. Members have a choice of single or joint coverage. Pre-existing condition limitations apply in many states.

Enrollment is simple and premiums are collected from the member with the loan payment. The cost is based on the outstanding loan balance. See figure 5.3 for a sample credit insurance application and schedule of benefits.

Member Services

CREDIT UNION LENDING

Figure 5.3 Credit Insurance Application

LOANLINER

CREDIT INSURANCE

You can protect your financial future by signing up for **voluntary** credit insurance below. Enroll by simply indicating your preference in the "Credit Insurance Application" section below. Your credit union will be happy to explain the various insurance options and coverage. The cost is reasonable.

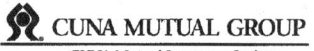

CUNA MUTUAL GROUP
CUNA Mutual Insurance Society
P.O. Box 391 • 5910 Mineral Point Road
Madison, WI 53701-0391
Phone: 800/937-2644

CREDIT INSURANCE APPLICATION & SCHEDULE

"You" or "Your" means the member and the joint insured (if applicable). A co-signor is not eligible for joint coverage.

Within 15 days after you receive the Certificate, you have the right to return the Certificate to the credit union for cancellation and any premium paid by you will be immediately returned.

Credit insurance **is voluntary and not required in order to obtain this loan.** You may select any insurer of your choice. You can get this insurance only if you check the "yes" box and sign your name and write in the date. The rate you are charged for the insurance is subject to change. You will receive written notice before any increase goes into effect. You have the right to stop this insurance by notifying your credit union in writing. Your signature below means you agree that:

- If you elect insurance, you authorize the credit union to add the charges for insurance to your loan each month.

- You are eligible for disability insurance only if you are working for wages or profit for 25 hours a week or more on the initial Loan Date. If you are not, you will not be insured until you return to work. If you are off work because of temporary layoff, strike or vacation, but soon to resume, you will be considered at work.

- You are eligible for insurance up to the Maximum Age for Insurance. Insurance will stop when you reach that age.

NOTE: THE LIFE AND DISABILITY INSURANCE CONTAINS CERTAIN BENEFIT EXCLUSIONS, INCLUDING A PRE-EXISTING CONDITION EXCLUSION. PLEASE REFER TO YOUR CERTIFICATE FOR DETAILS.

YOU ELECT THE FOLLOWING INSURANCE COVERAGE(S)	YES	NO	COST PER $100 OF YOUR MONTHLY LOAN BALANCE	COVERED MEMBER

If you are totally disabled for more than _____ days, then the disability benefit will begin with the _____ day of disability.

CREDIT UNION NAME AND ADDRESS

INSURANCE MAXIMUMS	DISABILITY	LIFE
MONTHLY TOTAL DISABILITY BENEFIT	$	N/A
INSURABLE BALANCE PER LOAN ACCOUNT	$	$
MAXIMUM AGE FOR INSURANCE		

MEMBER'S NAME AND ADDRESS

JOINT INSURED'S NAME AND ADDRESS

SECONDARY BENEFICIARY (If you desire to name one)

MEMBER'S ACCOUNT NUMBER | GROUP POLICY NUMBER | DATE OF ISSUE OF THE CERTIFICATE

DATE | SOCIAL SECURITY NUMBER | MEMBER'S DATE OF BIRTH | DATE | SOCIAL SECURITY NUMBER | JOINT INSURED'S DATE OF BIRTH

SIGNATURE OF MEMBER | SIGNATURE OF JOINT INSURED (CO-BORROWER)
(Only required if JOINT CREDIT LIFE or JOINT CREDIT DISABILITY coverage is selected)

APP.835-0496WI
© CUNA MUTUAL GROUP, 1980, 82, 84, 86, 89, 98, ALL RIGHTS RESERVED
IWI701 (LASER) 27860

Source: © CUNA Mutual Group, Madison, Wisconsin. Reprinted with permission.

Credit Disability Insurance

Credit disability insurance is another type of voluntary credit insurance that a majority of credit unions offer to working members. After a short waiting period (typically thirty days or less), **credit disability insurance** makes payments, up to the contract limit, when an insured member becomes totally disabled due to an accident or illness. Loss or reduction of income is a time of serious stress for most people. Credit disability helps the member cope financially while he or she recovers. It helps members keep their loans current, which reduces delinquencies, foreclosures, and collections. CUNA Mutual notes the following statistics that demonstrate the value of credit disability insurance:

- only 20 percent of the population has long-term disability coverage; the average benefit provided is 60 percent of salary;
- 48 percent of all foreclosures occur during a disability;
- 35 percent of CUNA Mutual Group disability claims are due to accidental causes.

Members may have a choice of joint coverage (where available) and retroactive or nonretroactive plans (for which there are waiting periods of fourteen or thirty days). Pre-existing condition limitations typically apply. The coverage stops when the loan is repaid, the member reaches the maximum age for the coverage, or the member dies.

As with credit life insurance, enrollment is easy and premiums are collected with the loan payment. The cost is based on the outstanding loan balance. The sample credit insurance application shown in figure 5.3 can also be used for credit disability insurance.

Now that you have reviewed basic concepts common to credit union loans, the next chapter discusses the different types of loans typically found at credit unions.

Complete activity 5.3 to review your knowledge of basic loan concepts covered in this chapter.

Member Services

CREDIT UNION LENDING

Activity 5.3 Building Your Knowledge of Loan Terminology

Match the statements in the second column with the terms in the first column.

___ 1. character
___ 2. unsecured loan
___ 3. open-end loan
___ 4. capacity
___ 5. secured loan
___ 6. closed-end loan
___ 7. collateral

a. one-time extension of credit
b. ability to repay a loan
c. something of value used to secure a loan
d. credit used on an on-going basis
e. indicated by credit report and other evidence of stability
f. collateral is provided for this type of loan
g. signature loan is an example

Answers appear in appendix A.

Chapter 6 Types of Loan Programs

Credit unions provide affordable loans to members. Because the credit union is not a for-profit business, loan rates are often lower than those offered by other financial institutions. Credit unions base loan decisions on the members' credit history, their ability to repay the loan, and the collateral available for security.

As described in chapter 5, loans are secured or unsecured. This chapter reviews typical features and benefits of these types of loans.

Types of Unsecured Loans

This section covers the different types of unsecured loans commonly found at credit unions:

- signature (personal) loans;
- lines of credit, including share draft overdraft protection;
- credit card accounts;
- education loans;
- business loans.

Signature Loans

As described in the previous chapter, signature loans were the first type of loans credit unions made. They are granted purely on the basis of the borrower's creditworthiness and are not secured by collateral. Rates on these type of loans are usually high (compared to other credit union loans) and the loans are closed-end.

Objectives

Upon completion of this chapter, you will be able to

1. **describe features and benefits of unsecured loans;**
2. **outline how a credit card transaction is processed;**
3. **describe features and benefits of secured loans;**
4. **differentiate purchase money loan and nonpurchase money loan;**
5. **describe the features of an automobile leasing program;**
6. **define** *lien, cap,* **and** *points* **in relation to a mortgage loan;**
7. **differentiate first and second mortgages;**
8. **calculate home equity and lendable equity;**
9. **explain when the right of rescission applies to home loans.**

For members who are young or have little credit history, the credit union may require a cosigner on a signature loan. A **cosigner** (guarantor) is an individual, not necessarily a member of the credit union, who agrees to sign a legal document guaranteeing the debt of the borrowing member. If the

TYPES OF LOAN PROGRAMS

borrower defaults, the cosigner is liable for the full amount of the loan and is obligated to pay the loan in full.

Members often use signature loans to pay bills, buy large-ticket items, or consolidate other loans to take advantage of low credit union rates. Credit union loans can help members avoid the higher cost of financing purchases, such as appliances or electronics, through the store selling the item.

Lines of Credit

To establish a personal **line of credit** for a member, the credit union determines the maximum amount the member qualifies for on his or her signature. The credit union accomplishes this by using the same criteria for creditworthiness as it does on signature loans. The credit union grants the member a pre-approved amount of credit, accessible at any time, up to the established credit limit, provided the member is not in default and remains creditworthy.

Another popular line of credit is the **overdraft protection** plan. It serves a dual purpose for members. It gives members even more convenient access to a line of credit loan and doubles as overdraft protection. The member merely writes a share draft to access the line of credit. Usually amounts are advanced in increments of not less than a certain dollar amount, for example, $50. Thus, if Michael writes a draft for $170 when he has only $150 in his account, the credit union will automatically transfer $50 into his share draft account and add $50 to the line of credit loan balance. Payments on line of credit loans are normally set up on monthly installments.

For members, overdraft protection plans give quick and easy emergency cash or cash for special purchases. When a member finds a bargain but doesn't have the cash on hand, the line of credit allows the member to make the purchase on the spot.

By establishing pre-approved lines of credit for members, credit unions enhance member convenience and reduce paperwork that would otherwise be caused by repeated loan requests.

Complete activity 6.1 to find out about your credit union's overdraft protection plan.

Credit Card Accounts

Many credit unions offer credit cards to their members. Many members consider credit cards to be a financial necessity. Members use credit cards to make everyday purchases. Most business establishments accept credit cards. Even charities, health professionals, and attorneys routinely offer the option of paying with credit cards.

Administration of Credit Card Accounts and Transactions

When a credit union offers a Visa or MasterCard program, it pays a licensing fee for the use of the name. In essence, the credit union is buying the name recognition and acceptance factor of the card program (not unlike

Member Services

TYPES OF LOAN PROGRAMS

Activity 6.1 Increasing Your Knowledge of Overdraft Protection

Find out about your credit union's overdraft protection plan (if available) and answer the following questions.

1. What interest rate is charged?

2. How does a member apply for overdraft protection?

3. How does the member make payments?

4. How is this member service promoted at your credit union?

---

purchasing a fast food restaurant franchise). However, the credit union has considerable leeway to customize the program.

Credit unions often contract with specialized data processing operations to provide some or all of the data processing services required to support their credit card programs. These services include generating credit card statements, processing and posting payments, and handling credit limit approvals.

After applying for a credit card, a member is approved for a maximum credit limit based on an evaluation of his or her creditworthiness. Credit is extended on a revolving basis, meaning the amount of credit available is determined by subtracting the outstanding balance from the approved credit line. The amount of credit is replenished as soon as a payment is made.

Once the application is approved, the card processor establishes an account for the member and issues the credit card. The credit union member usually receives the card in the mail and must follow a card activation process before using it. This provides a measure of security against unauthorized use of the card.

Members can then begin using the card to make purchases on credit. After a sale is completed, the merchant's bank account receives a credit for the face amount of the purchase less a negotiated discount (as a fee).

The merchant receives several benefits from accepting a credit card. The merchant pays the small fee because he or she would rather be sure of collecting a slightly smaller amount on a credit card payment than take a chance on accepting a check that may be fraudulent. The merchant benefits by allowing customers access to credit without establishing a costly system of his or her own, and by not having to handle and maintain as much cash at the checkout area. Access to credit also generates extra sales from impulse buyers and travelers.

In addition to using credit cards for purchases, members can also use credit cards to receive cash advances at thousands of locations. This makes credit cards an excellent resource for emergencies. Also, many members find that credit cards come in handy for use as supplementary identification.

Repayment Terms and Grace Periods

Repayment on credit card accounts is made on a monthly basis. A minimum monthly payment is required. For example, a credit union could set the minimum payment as $20 or 3 percent of the outstanding balance, whichever is greater. Due to the card's revolving credit structure, there is no established payoff date, but members have the option of paying the balance off in full each month.

The manner in which the finance charge is calculated can vary from one credit union to another. Some programs impose a finance charge from the date the credit card purchase is posted. This type of card is called a nongrace card. The other option offers a grace period (usually twenty-five days). The member can pay the balance in full before the due date without incurring any finance charges.

Some credit cards have a grace period and some do not. A **grace period** is the time between the date of a purchase and the date interest starts being charged on that purchase. If the card has a standard grace period, the member has an opportunity to avoid finance charges by paying the current balance in full. Some issuers allow a grace period for new purchases even if the member does not pay the balance in full every month. If there is no grace period, the issuer imposes a finance charge from the date the member uses the card or from the date each transaction is posted to the member's account.

Many credit unions offer both grace and nongrace cards to appeal to different segments of their membership. For the many credit cardholders who do not pay their balances off in full each month, a nongrace card with a lower rate of interest is appealing. However, for those members who pay in full, a program with a grace period, regardless of the interest rate, is more attractive.

See figure 6.1 for a sample description of credit card programs at one credit union.

Figure 6.1 Sample Credit Card Programs

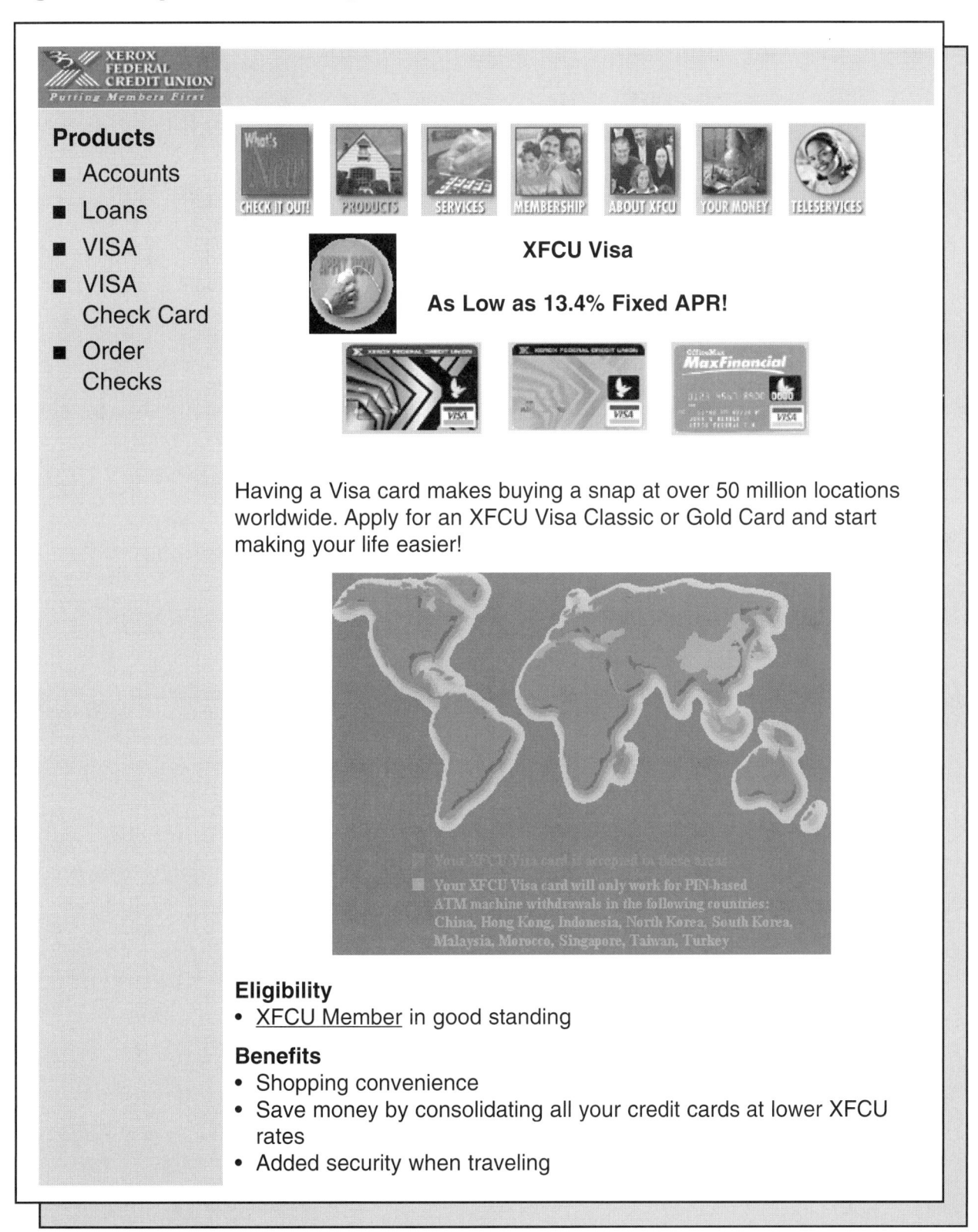

Products
- Accounts
- Loans
- VISA
- VISA Check Card
- Order Checks

XFCU Visa

As Low as 13.4% Fixed APR!

Having a Visa card makes buying a snap at over 50 million locations worldwide. Apply for an XFCU Visa Classic or Gold Card and start making your life easier!

Eligibility
- XFCU Member in good standing

Benefits
- Shopping convenience
- Save money by consolidating all your credit cards at lower XFCU rates
- Added security when traveling

Source: © Xerox Federal Credit Union, El Segundo, California. Reprinted with permission.

Member Services

TYPES OF LOAN PROGRAMS

Figure 6.1 Sample Credit Card Programs (Continued)

Features
- Low fixed interest rates
- No fee for cash advances
- 25 day grace period on all retail purchases
- Cash advances from ATMs worldwide
- Free travel/accident coverage when purchasing travel tickets
- AirMiles Option—Earn points towards free airline tickets! No blackout periods, no Saturday night stayovers required, and international flights are allowed!
- Gold cards only—Emergency Replacement within 24 hours if the card is lost or stolen. The phone number to replace a lost or stolen card is (800) 449-7728.

XFCU offers a variety of Visa programs. There's one that's right for you. Apply today!

VISA TYPE	INTEREST RATE/ANNUAL FEE	MAX. CREDIT LIMIT	MIN. PMT*	TRAVEL/ ACC. INS.
Classic	14.4%/NONE	$10,000	$20.00 or 3% of bal.	Free up to $200,000
Gold	13.4%/$25	$25,000	$20.00 or 2.5% of bal.	Free up to $500,000
AirMiles Option Classic	14.4%/$25	$10,000	$20.00 or 3% of bal.	Free up to $200,000
AirMiles Option Gold	13.4%/$50	$25,000	$20.00 or 3% of bal.	Free up to $500,000
Secured**	16.9%/None	$5,000	$20.00 or 4% of bal.	None

*Greater of the two.
**Secured by 100% of the funds in a Share Secured Club Account

HOME　　BRANCH LOCATIONS　　ATM LOCATIONS　　RATES　　APPLY NOW　　CALCULATORS　　SEARCH

TYPES OF LOAN PROGRAMS

Fees

Different fees apply to credit card accounts. Some credit unions charge an annual fee for a credit card while others do not. Of the credit unions that do, the fee usually ranges from $20 to $40 a year. These fees are not finance charges, but a fee paid just for carrying the card. Some cards with prestige features have higher annual fees.

Some credit unions charge a fee to members who exceed their approved credit limit. Members are usually notified of over-extension, and the credit union will generally expect the members to make a payment and bring the balance back down under the limit.

Some credit unions charge a late fee when the payment is received after the due date. Others do not charge a late fee.

Prestige Features

Prestige features are becoming more common with many card programs. The originator of the prestige or status card is American Express. The original American Express green card, and subsequent gold and platinum cards, were marketed as status symbols to convey exclusivity for their cardholders.

Other attractions of the status cards are the special services attached to them. These services can include rental car insurance, road assistance, purchase assurance (an insurance program that protects cardholders when damaged or stolen items were purchased using the card), extended warranties on items purchased with the card, and product discounts. Credit unions, again in addressing the varying needs of their different membership segments, have capitalized on this idea. Many now offer Visa or MasterCard accounts with many of these specialized services.

Complete activity 6.2 to learn more about your credit union's credit card program.

Education Loans

Many credit unions also offer government guaranteed loans for educational purposes. The most widely used loans are the Federal Family Education Loan (FFEL) Stafford Loans and the Federal Family Education Loan (FFEL) PLUS Loans.

With the FFEL Stafford Loan program, the loan has a term of ten years and the student has a choice of three repayment plans:

- a fixed payment amount each month;
- a payment that is lower at the start of the loan and then increases over time;
- a payment that is sensitive to the student's yearly income and loan amount. Payments change as income rises and falls.

The FFEL PLUS Loans enable parents with good credit histories to borrow to pay the education expenses of each child who is a dependent undergraduate student enrolled at least half time. The interest rate on the loan is variable with an interest rate cap. The interest rate is adjusted on an annual basis. A minimum of $600

Member Services

TYPES OF LOAN PROGRAMS

Activity 6.2 Learning about Credit Card Programs at Your Credit Union

Find out about your credit union's credit card program to answer the following questions:

1. What credit card program does your credit union offer (if any)?
   _____

2. What interest rate is charged on the credit card?
   _____

3. Does the account have a grace period?
   _____

4. What annual fee is charged (if any)?
   _____

5. How does a member apply for a credit card?
   _____

---

must be repaid annually and the loan has a term of ten years.

Credit unions that offer education loans usually have a specialist on their staff to whom you will refer members.

Business Loans

Service to businesses is a growing area at many credit unions. Credit unions that make business loans are responding to members' needs. Just as members need a convenient, low-cost source of consumer funds, many also need funding for small business enterprises and equipment. Members may want to obtain business loans for a variety of purposes. (These types of loans may be unsecured or secured.) Examples of unsecured loans include loans to buy into a franchise and loans for operating expenses. The creditworthiness of the business and the owner is critical for unsecured loans.

Business lending is a complex field and requires specialized, experienced lenders. It is, however, an area of service that more and more credit unions are exploring—and one with which you should become familiar. Check with your credit union's lending department to find out if

> Service to businesses is a growing area at many credit unions.

88

your credit union offers loans to businesses and what the typical reasons and amounts are for the loans.

Types of Secured Loans

The other major category of loans at credit unions is secured loans (loans secured by collateral). There are two categories of these loans:

- purchase money loans;
- nonpurchase money loans.

Purchase money loans are secured by whatever is purchased with the loan proceeds. When a member applies for an automobile loan, the car will normally be used to secure the loan. Other examples are loans to purchase boats, campers, or motorcycles. Or, if a member obtains a home loan to purchase a house, the property is the collateral that secures the loan.

A **collateralized nonpurchase money loan** is secured with an item already owned by the member. The member uses the loan proceeds for a purpose unrelated to the purchase of the item. For example, a member could use a share certificate as collateral for a loan. Consider another example. Janet needs to pay medical bills. She has a mortgage on her home but has paid down the loan sufficiently that she has built up a percentage of ownership (equity) in the home. Janet can use this equity to secure a loan to pay the bills.

Secured personal loans fall into the category of nonpurchase money loans. Often, credit unions will ask for collateral on personal loans if the member would not qualify for the entire amount requested on his or her signature alone, or if the amount requested exceeds the credit union's signature limit. These loans are called secured personal loans. For instance, John wants to borrow money to take a vacation but does not have a very long credit history. However, John owns his two-year old car and uses it as security for the loan.

The types of secured loans covered in this section are:

- vehicle loans and other options;
- first mortgage loans;
- home equity loans;
- home equity lines of credit;
- other secured loans such as share account loans, and stock loans.

Vehicle Loans and Other Options

A member can obtain a loan on a vehicle or lease it. In addition, some credit unions offer "lease look-alike" loans.

Vehicle Loans

Various types of vehicles can be used to secure a loan. Automobile loans are traditionally a mainstay of credit union lending. Both new and used vehicles can be financed at attractive rates. For new vehicles, terms up to five years are often available. To compete with dealer financing and other sources of automobile loans, credit unions have developed

TYPES OF LOAN PROGRAMS

several methods of responding to members' needs:

- **Fast approval on loan requests.** Underwriters need to give a quick response so the member knows if he or she can get the car desired.

- **Preapproval.** Members can apply for a loan without having already picked out a car. The credit union preapproves the member for credit and gives the member a certificate that shows the member has been preapproved for a loan up to a certain amount. In this way, the member can shop for a car with the certificate in hand. A dealer may be more willing to offer the best deal when they know the member has been preapproved.

- **Financing at the dealer.** Some credit unions have established arrangements with dealers so that individuals can obtain credit union financing at the dealership. Nonmembers can become members at the dealership.

Members can also obtain credit union loans for RVs, boats, motorcycles, camping trailers, and even aircraft.

In general, the vehicle serves as collateral for the loan. For most vehicles, the credit union establishes the security interest by being registered as a lienholder on the certificate of title, which is the ownership document. Certificates of title are usually filed with the secretary of state or other department of the state government. A **lien** is a claim that a party has on the property of another party as security for payment of a debt or outstanding bill. When the loan is paid off, the credit union releases the lien. If the loan is not paid off, the credit union has the legal right to take the vehicle and sell it.

Automobile Leasing

As an alternative to buying a vehicle, consumers may lease them. Due to consumer demand, some credit unions offer automobile leasing plans. Although these are not loans, they are described here so that you can see their relationship to auto loans.

Essentially, here is how a leasing arrangement works. The consumer is not "renting" the car. He or she arranges for the car to be sold to a leasing company (often an arm of the dealership or other company that specializes in these arrangements). The consumer pays little or no money as a down payment. The leasing company then allows the consumer to drive the car for a monthly charge for a set number of years. The term is usually two or three years but it can be longer. Leases usually have annual mileage limitations, such as 15,000 miles (with a cents-per-mile charge for excess mileage). When the lease period is up, the consumer can simply return the car or purchase it at the **residual value,** which is the value of the car as agreed upon at the start of the lease. For example, the lease might state that a particular car purchased for $20,000 has a residual value of $5,000 at the end of the lease (depending on the model of the car and the length of the lease).

Leasing has benefits and drawbacks for consumers. Primary benefits of leasing are a lower monthly payment than a loan and the ability to get a new car every few years without the hassle of selling the old one. Drawbacks primarily center around getting a good deal on the lease. How the lease payment and residual value are calculated can be complex and difficult to understand. Without careful shopping, a consumer can end up paying more on a lease than a loan. In fact, the Federal Reserve now requires dealers to give shoppers a one-page document that discloses key terms about a lease: residual value, interest rate, length of the lease, and the size of the down payment, if any. As leasing becomes more widespread and matures as a financial product for consumers, the shopping methods and comparisons should become better understood.

"Lease Look-Alike" Loans

As an alternative to leasing, some credit unions have introduced auto loans based on leasing principles. This is not an actual leasing program, but a variation of the conventional auto loan.

For a "lease look-alike" loan, members choose a date when they ideally want to trade in the new financed vehicle for their next new car (such as one, two, or three years). Using that term, the credit union determines the value of the financed car at that trade-in time. (To determine this amount, the credit union uses a valuation book that leasing agencies commonly use.)

The credit union calculates payments on the loan so that at the end of the specified term, the car's value and the loan balance are equal, giving the member zero equity in the car. One of the benefits resulting from this type of loan plan is that the member's payments are much lower than those of a conventional auto loan.

At the end of the "lease-like" term, the credit union can give the member several options. For example, the member could sell the vehicle and pay off the residual value, trade for a new car and pay the residual value as part of the transaction, or refinance the residual value as a used vehicle loan. The member also has the option to return the vehicle. In this case, some credit unions simply require the member to

- pay any excess mileage charges;
- return the vehicle with all original equipment;
- repair any damage insurance has not paid for.

In addition, the credit union holds an insurance policy that guarantees the value of the car at the end of the loan so no loss is taken if the actual residual value is lower than expected.

> Primary benefits of leasing are a lower monthly payment than a loan and the ability to get a new car every few years without the hassle of selling the old one.

TYPES OF LOAN PROGRAMS

First Mortgage Loans

Mortgage loans are made on any type of real estate. For credit unions, their primary market is home mortgage loans.

Home ownership has been called the "American dream." The thought of owning a home has a powerful emotional draw for many members. They are proud of achieving homeownership and enjoy stamping their own personalities and preferences on their homes. They also perceive their homes as financial investments because well-maintained homes have a long tradition of appreciating in value over time. Members feel that their monthly loan payments are increasing their investment rather than being lost to rent.

Federal and state governments recognize the desire for homeownership by providing incentives to make it possible for more people. They make mortgage interest on our homes generally tax-deductible and sponsor or encourage loan programs that increase the numbers of people who are eligible for home ownership. Efforts such as these have helped the rate of homeownership increase in our nation (see figure 6.2).

Credit unions strongly support initiatives to make home ownership available to more people. One of the ways they encourage home ownership is by providing residential mortgage loans at attractive interest rates. Mortgage loans give credit unions a long-term relationship with members, increasing their loyalty and predisposition to do additional business with the credit union in the future. In fact, when a member has good experiences with a mortgage loan, that relationship can have more importance to building loyalty than a checking account.

Real Estate Value and Loan Amount

Loans secured by real estate are, as a rule, solid loans. Mortgage loans use real estate (real property) as collateral. A mortgage on real estate is like a lien on a car's title, as discussed earlier. If your credit union makes a first mortgage loan on real estate, it has the primary claim, or **first lien,** to the real estate should the loan go into default. The lien is usually recorded in a government department in the county where the real estate is located. Recording the lien puts notice in public records that the credit union has first lien to the property.

Before the credit union lends against any type of real estate it must estimate the current value. This gives the credit union an indication of what the value would be if it were sold upon foreclosure. To determine the market value of real estate, the credit union obtains a detailed report from a qualified appraiser whose profession is the valuation of real estate.

The thought of owning a home has a powerful emotional draw for many members.

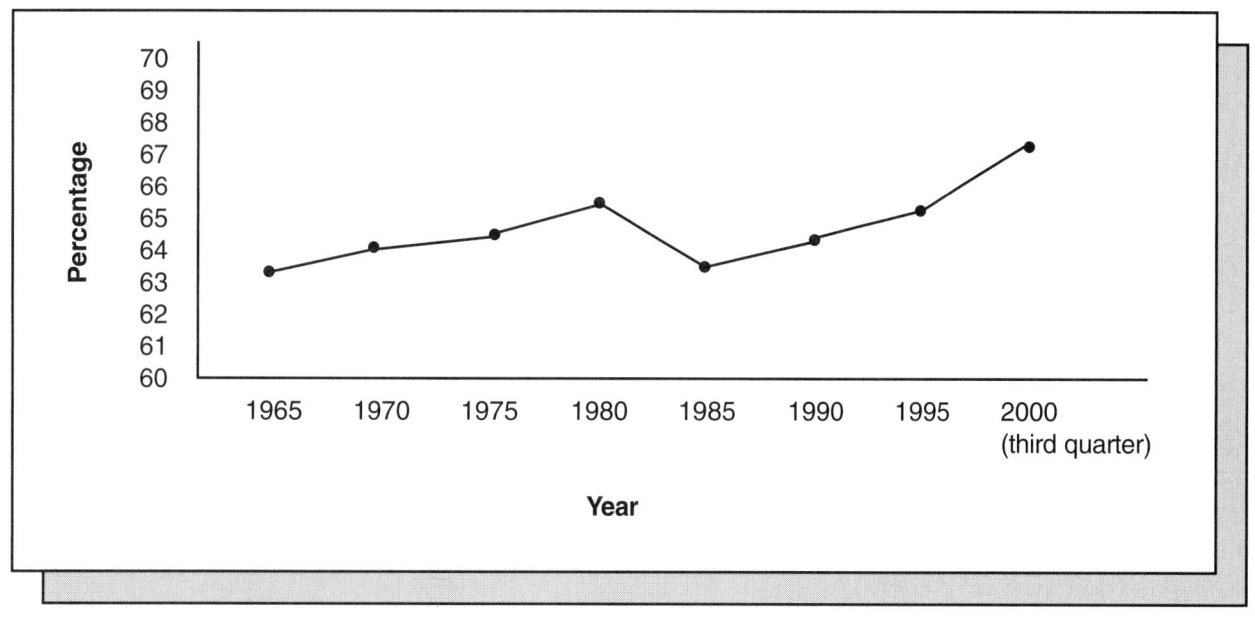

Figure 6.2 Homeownership Rates for the United States

Source: U.S. Census Bureau

After obtaining a market value, the credit union can determine how much it will lend on the real estate. The amount of the first mortgage loan will often be as high as 80 to 90 percent of the value. (Some special programs, such as government-sponsored programs, may allow a loan for a higher percentage.)

Loan Underwriting

In addition to obtaining a market value for the real estate, the credit union considers other factors when evaluating the loan request. As discussed in the last chapter, the creditworthiness of the member is critical in this process. Due to the large amount invested in a mortgage loan, the loan underwriter looks at a wide variety of information about a borrower when reviewing the loan request.

Loan Terms and Rates

Terms of first mortgage loans vary and are highly sensitive to market rates. A typical first mortgage loan is set up for fifteen to thirty years on monthly installments. Interest rates can be either fixed or variable. Many credit union mortgage loans are fixed rate and closed-end, especially when the loan is made for a purchase money loan. As mentioned earlier, a closed-end loan is one with a specified maturity date.

Member Services

TYPES OF LOAN PROGRAMS

Credit unions also are likely to offer **adjustable rate mortgages (ARMs).** An ARM is a mortgage on which the interest rate can fluctuate, much like the variable-rate loans discussed in chapter 5. ARMs enable credit unions and members to more equitably share the risks and benefits of changing market rates.

With an ARM, the interest rate of the loan can be increased or decreased without rewriting the loan. Usually an interest rate limit, or **cap,** is stated, and when the property is a dwelling (under the federal Truth-in-Lending Act) the loan *must* have a life-of-the-loan cap. For example, the loan terms could limit the interest rate increase to 2 percent per year, and 5 percent over the life of the loan.

Loan Fees

Various fees apply to mortgage loans. Most of these fees are collected when the loan is "closed." This is the point when the loan proceeds are paid out and the member begins making payments.

Most mortgage loans are subject to points. **Points** are a one-time charge, sometimes called a loan origination fee, that are calculated as a percentage of the loan amount. Each point charged equals 1 percent of the principal amount of the loan. The number of points charged is usually between one and four, though it can be higher. For instance, a member who is financing a $100,000 mortgage at two points would pay $2,000 as part of the closing costs of the loan.

Other closing costs members typically pay, which are common to mortgage loans, include:

- **Appraisal fee.** The appraiser charges this fee for estimating the market value of the real estate. Appraisals vary in cost, depending on how extensively the appraiser must research the property. Fees can range from $50 to $500.

- **Mortgage registration and/or transfer taxes.** These costs vary from county to county.

- **Filing fee.** This is a fee for the filing and handling of the mortgage document with the county.

- **Credit report.** Some credit unions charge for credit reports that they obtain to qualify members for the loan.

- **Fees for title examination.** This fee is paid for an examination of public records to make sure the property does not have any other liens on it or other problems with ownership.

Home Equity Loans

Typically, members obtain a first mortgage loan when they purchase real estate. The cost of most types of residential and other real estate is sufficiently high that members would have a difficult time saving enough money to purchase the property outright.

Members may also obtain mortgage loans on a nonpurchase money basis. For example, some

Member Services

TYPES OF LOAN PROGRAMS

time after obtaining a first mortgage loan, the member may have a need to borrow money for some other purpose. Or, a member may own a home without a mortgage but has a need to borrow money. In these cases, credit unions may make what is usually called a home equity loan. **Home equity loans** are a type of mortgage loan that uses residential real estate as collateral for a loan that may be a first or second mortgage.

A **second mortgage** is a loan made on real estate that already has a first mortgage. A first mortgage has priority over a second mortgage in case of loan default and foreclosure. If your credit union holds a second mortgage, it is second in line for rights to the member's property in case of default. For example, assume that State Bank of Lincoln City holds the first mortgage on a member's home. Your credit union holds a second mortgage. The member is not making payments to the credit union on the second mortgage. After your credit union forecloses on the property, it would have to pay off the loan at State Bank of Lincoln City before it would have the legal right to sell the property and pay off the second mortgage.

Members usually obtain home equity loans when they want a large loan and they have enough equity in their home to use it as security for the loan. Major home improvements and large bill consolidations are two common uses for home equity loans.

Equity and Loan Amount

The amount a credit union lends on a home equity loan depends on the amount of equity the member has in his or her home, and your credit union's loan policies. **Equity** is the difference between the home's appraised value (which is determined by a qualified appraiser) and the existing mortgage balance, if any. If the property has no mortgage, then the member's equity is 100 percent of the appraised value of the home. Usually a credit union will lend a percentage, say 90 percent, of the member's equity (less the mortgage balance). The percentage the credit union lends against is determined by its lending policies.

A member's equity is increased in two ways:

1. The home's value has appreciated since its purchase, which means it is worth more now than when it was purchased. The value may have risen due to overall increases in home values in the area or the member may have improved the property in ways that increase value.

2. The member has paid on the first mortgage loan for several years, or has otherwise reduced the balance considerably. For example, perhaps the member received an inheritance a few years ago and used it to pay down the balance of the mortgage loan, thereby increasing his or her equity.

TYPES OF LOAN PROGRAMS

The following example illustrates how equity and a loan amount are calculated. Assume that a home was purchased for $125,000 a number of years ago. Today, the home is appraised at $150,000. The home has a first mortgage balance of $100,000. The credit union's maximum loan amount is 90 percent of equity. Here is how the equity and a maximum home equity loan balance are calculated:

Appraised value	$150,000
Multiply (x) by 90%	x 90%
	$135,000
Minus (-) existing mortgage	- 100,000
Lendable equity	$ 35,000

Home Equity Loan Features

Home equity loans and first mortgage loans have similarities and differences. Interest rates on home equity loans are usually higher than those of first mortgage loans. Some credit unions offer lower rates when the equity percentage is lower. For example, a credit union would offer a lower rate of interest on a loan that is calculated at 50 percent of the equity versus 80 percent of equity. These loans can be set up as fixed or variable rates.

The term of repayment is shorter on home equity loans. The term is often ten to fifteen years, although the term can be considerably shorter if the borrowed amount is relatively small.

Closing costs for home equity loans are also less than those of first mortgages. It is rare to find points charged on a home equity loan. However, the member is charged for standard appraisal and filing fees.

Right of Rescission

The right of rescission applies to some types of mortgage loans. The **right of rescission** means that the member has three business days to cancel, or rescind, the loan obligation after signing the loan documents. This means that (for certain types of mortgage loans) the funds cannot be disbursed on the same day the loan papers are signed. If the member rescinds, all charges in connection with the mortgage transaction must be refunded.

When does the right of rescission apply? It applies to loans that give a security interest in the member's principal residence *except* when the loan is a residential purchase money mortgage. In other words, if the member obtains a mortgage loan to purchase a principal residence, the right of rescission does not apply. It *does* apply to home equity loans where the member's principal residence secures the loan and no purchase is involved.

Member Benefits of Home Equity Loans

Members enjoy several benefits from home equity loans. The interest rate is significantly lower than credit cards and personal, unsecured loans. It may be lower than a long-term automobile loan because homes usually retain value better than vehicles over the long-term.

Member Services

TYPES OF LOAN PROGRAMS

The primary benefit most members value is the possible tax deduction of mortgage interest from income taxes (under some restrictions). For this reason, some members may use a home equity loan for a purpose such as purchasing a car or some other large expense. Members also may consolidate credit card debt and convert it to home equity debt for this reason. Members must consult a tax advisor or make their own determination as to whether they would enjoy tax benefits from a home equity loan, however. Credit union employees do not provide tax advice.

Home Equity Lines of Credit

Home equity lines of credit (HELOCs) are a type of home equity credit that operates much like a personal line of credit. The difference is that instead of being secured only by the member's signature, the credit union takes an additional mortgage or security interest on the member's home. The amount the credit union pre-approves on a HELOC is calculated on a percentage of the member's equity in his or her home. This calculation is done in the same manner as that of home equity loans.

As with home equity loans, members obtain HELOCs for a variety of reasons (see figure 6.3). The primary use is to pay for home improvements, such as kitchen remodeling, additions, and major repairs.

Once approved, the member receives advances on the line of credit whenever and for whatever purpose. Members can access this line of credit directly through the credit union. It is also common to tie the loan to a share draft account or credit card for the member's convenience. Sometimes the credit union establishes a minimum advance limit, usually $1,000 or more.

Home equity lines of credit represent the ultimate in convenience for many members, and also enable them to receive the benefit of tax deductions. Benefits to the credit union include a steady source of loan demand, with solid collateral and a minimum of processing/staff time.

Terms on these loans vary, depending on the amount of equity, the amount preapproved, and the extent to which the member borrows against the line of credit. Payments are usually established by calculating a percentage of each $500 (or less, depending upon the credit union's minimum advance policy) outstanding on the loan, or a minimum payment amount (usually around $75), whichever is greater.

Interest rates on HELOCs are usually comparable to or slightly lower than home equity loans, and repayment is made on a monthly basis. It is rare for points to be charged on a HELOC. Closing costs are similar to those of home equity loans.

Home equity lines of credit represent the ultimate in convenience for many members, and also enable them to receive the benefit of tax deductions.

Member Services
TYPES OF LOAN PROGRAMS

Figure 6.3 Uses of Home Equity Lines of Credit

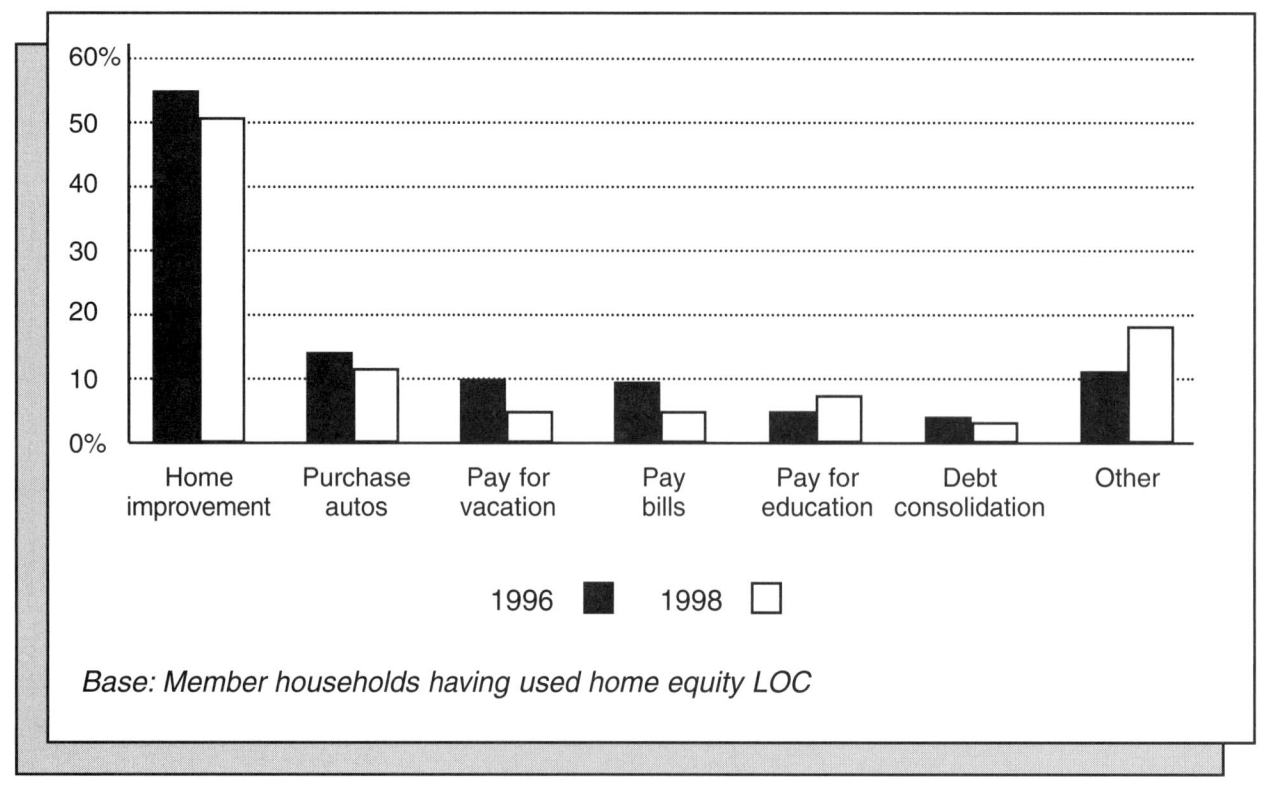

Category	1996	1998
Home improvement	55%	51%
Purchase autos	14%	11%
Pay for vacation	10%	5%
Pay bills	10%	5%
Pay for education	5%	7%
Debt consolidation	4%	3%
Other	11%	18%

Base: Member households having used home equity LOC

Source: *1998 National Member Survey, Credit Union Magazine,* CUNA & Affiliates, Madison, Wisconsin.

See figure 6.4 for an example of home equity loan programs.

Complete activity 6.3 to learn more about your credit union's mortgage and home equity loans.

Other Secured Loans

Credit unions may make other types of secured loans. One example is **share account loans.** A credit union secures a portion or all of a loan with a savings account at the credit union. Many times the credit union offers the loan at a reduced rate if it is fully secured by savings. When a member has credit problems but wants to reestablish his or credit rating, a share-secured loan is sometimes the only type the credit union will make. However, you should note that IRAs cannot be pledged as collateral for a loan.

A credit union can also make a loan and hold a member's shares of stock in a company as collateral. Securities can be fairly solid collateral as long as their value can be determined. These loans are more frequently made at a credit union where a large employee group works at a company where employees participate in a stock purchase plan. The value of the stock is closely monitored and if the value declines, borrowers may need to pledge more shares of stock against the loan or pay down part of the balance.

Member Services

TYPES OF LOAN PROGRAMS

Figure 6.4 Sample Home Equity Loan Programs

Home Equity Loans are the consumer loans where the interest may be tax deductible*.

Use a Rogue Federal Credit Union Home Equity Loan however you want and you could be able to deduct up to 100% of the interest.

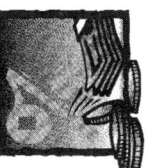

There are three ways for you to take advantage of the equity in your home at Rogue Federal Credit Union.

HOME EQUITY LINE OF CREDIT (HOMELINE)
- Pre-authorized credit line to draw on as needed
- Convenient, fast, easy access over the phone or through Call-24
- Competitive variable rates and fees
- Interest may be tax deductible*
- Finance up to 80% of established value less the 1st mortgage
- No pre-payment penalty
- Loan Protection Insurance Available— Life or Disability

SINGLE ADVANCE HOME EQUITY LOAN
- No pre-payment penalties
- Competitive fixed or variable rates
- Interest may be tax deductible*
- Finance up to 80% of established value less the 1st mortgage
- Terms up to 15 years
- Loan Protection Insurance Available—Life or Disability

MOBILE HOME ON LAND/PARK LOANS
- Competitive interest rates
- Short processing period
- No pre-payment penalty
- Flexible down payment and terms
- Loan Protection Insurance Available—Life or Disability

*Consult your tax advisor regarding your tax situation to determine tax deductibility.

DOCUMENTS NEEDED TO GET APPLICATION IN PROCESS
- Verification of income: Current check stub and previous year's W-2 If self-employed, last two years' tax returns
- County tax statement
- Most current statement from 1st Mortgage holder
- Copy of home owners insurance
- Completed application
- Registration information for mobile home loans

It's Easy To ESTIMATE Your Equity

	EXAMPLE	YOUR HOME
CURRENT VALUE OF YOUR HOME	$80,000	$ _____
MULTIPLY (×) BY 80%	× .80	× .80
EQUALS (=)	$64,000	$ _____
MINUS (−) EXISTING MORTGAGE	−$25,000	$ _____
EQUALS (=) LENDABLE EQUITY	$39,000	$ _____

SO PICK UP THE PHONE TODAY AND CALL OUR MORTGAGE DEPARTMENT

With one call, you can discover even greater value in your home, and determine which of these three options best fits your needs. **Call (541)858-7330 or 858-7328** Or simply send us the attached response slip.

Source: © Rogue Federal Credit Union, Medford, Oregon. Reprinted with permission.

Member Services

TYPES OF LOAN PROGRAMS

Activity 6.3 Developing Your Knowledge of Mortgage and Home Equity Loans

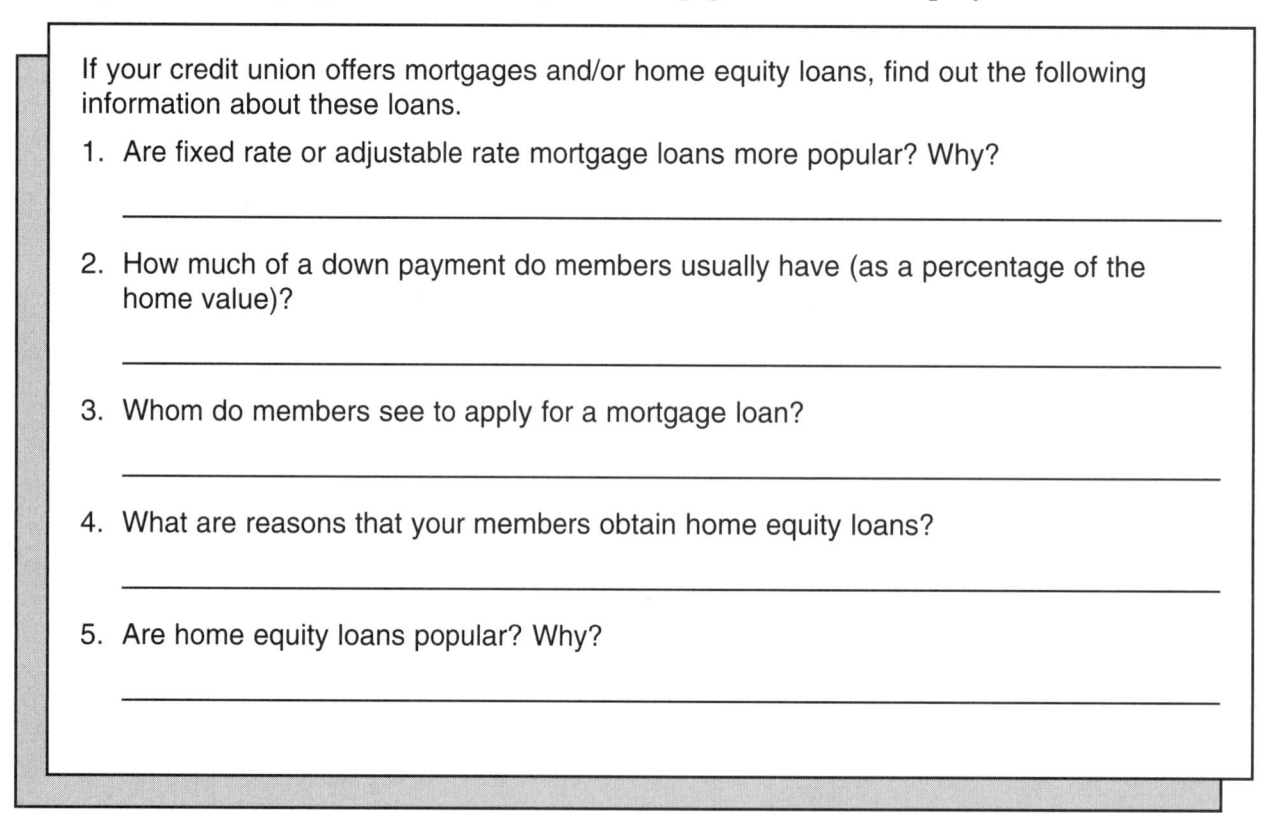

> If your credit union offers mortgages and/or home equity loans, find out the following information about these loans.
>
> 1. Are fixed rate or adjustable rate mortgage loans more popular? Why?
>   _____
>
> 2. How much of a down payment do members usually have (as a percentage of the home value)?
>   _____
>
> 3. Whom do members see to apply for a mortgage loan?
>   _____
>
> 4. What are reasons that your members obtain home equity loans?
>   _____
>
> 5. Are home equity loans popular? Why?
>   _____

Other types of personal property may be used as collateral for a loan. Examples include jewelry or coin collections. The difficulty with these items is determining their value as collateral.

Business loans may be secured by items such as equipment, real estate, or inventory. Agricultural loans may be collateralized by farm equipment, livestock, or crops. Some businesses, such as farms or retail businesses have seasonal needs for credit. Farmers need credit to plant crops and purchase livestock. When they sell the crops and livestock, farmers can repay the loan. Some types of retail businesses make the bulk of their profits during the winter holiday season. These business owners may borrow funds to purchase a large amount of inventory shortly before the holiday season and repay the loan after the inventory is sold. These are all specialized types of lending that require particular expertise in working with these types of collateral.

Complete activity 6.4 to learn more about your credit union's loan programs.

100

Member Services

TYPES OF LOAN PROGRAMS

Activity 6.4 Developing Knowledge of Your Credit Union's Loan Programs

Find out about loan programs at your credit union and the competition and answer the following questions.

1. How do your credit union's loan programs compare to your competition in terms of rates and other requirements? What are your credit union's competitive advantages?

   _____

   _____

2. Has your credit union recently advertised or otherwise promoted a particular loan program? What features and benefits were emphasized? What were the results of the promotion?

   _____

   _____

   _____

   _____

101

Chapter 7 Transaction Systems

We can certainly agree that credit unions are constantly looking at new types of services to add to their product lines. For example, the types of savings accounts have expanded over the years to include certificates of deposit and money market accounts. Also, credit unions are long past the days they only offered personal loans. They now offer a wide range of loan types. And, credit unions offer many other services that help members better manage their money.

However, in today's world of credit unions, the most revolutionary changes are taking place in how members access credit union services. Not so long ago, members had to physically come to a credit union office or use the mail to conduct any transactions. Then, credit unions began offering share draft accounts and electronic transfers. Members experienced the freedom of using their accounts away from the credit union office. From that point on, members wanted more and more convenient ways of conducting their financial transactions and credit unions have responded.

Today, members have many choices for transaction systems. You may hear marketing staff members refer to "multiple delivery channels" and "24/7

Objectives

Upon completion of this chapter, you will be able to

1. describe the features and member benefits of using direct deposit, automatic bill payment, and credit union transfers;

2. define *voice response unit* and explain the features and member benefits of telephone services;

3. differentiate ATM and debit card services and how they benefit members;

4. list the types of services available on credit union Internet web sites and how they can integrate with other transaction systems;

5. explain how members value personal service and how it eases their use of different types of transaction systems.

access" when they talk about how members access their accounts. This chapter covers the many options members now have for accessing their accounts and conducting their financial business. These options include ones that have been around for many years and others recently introduced:

- automatic transfers;
- telephone services;
- ATM and debit cards;
- Internet-based credit union services.

Automatic Transfers

For repetitive transactions, many members sign up for automatic deposits and payments. With these systems, funds are transferred between accounts at other financial institutions and the member's account at the credit union. Or, funds may be transferred between accounts at the credit union. Members like the time-saving convenience of the automatic transfer while avoiding worry of a check lost in the mail. The most popular services are direct deposit, automatic bill payment, and credit union account transfers.

Direct Deposit

With **direct deposit,** funds are automatically transferred from another institution to the member's credit union account. For example, members can arrange for their payroll amounts to be automatically deposited into their savings or share draft accounts. The employee receives a pay stub rather than a check from the employer and the deposit appears on the account statement. With payroll deduction, employees can arrange that only a portion of their pay is credited to a credit union savings or loan account. Some members have government recurring checks, such as federal retirement, social security benefits, and veteran's benefits direct deposited.

Automatic Bill Payment

With **automatic bill payment,** the member arranges for certain payments to be made automatically from their share draft accounts. This service pays a members' regularly recurring bills, such as insurance premiums, utility bills, and even television satellite-dish bills. The member signs a release form, which authorizes the credit union to pay specific creditors. When that creditor requests payment, the credit union can send the payment automatically. A notation that the payment was made is included on the member's monthly statement. The creditor usually sends a notification to the member in advance of the payment so that the member will remember to note it in a share draft account register.

Credit Union Account Transfers

Credit unions offer their members many systems for automatically transferring funds between accounts at the credit union. A popular choice is an automatic loan payment plan that transfers a loan payment automatically from a share draft account to a loan account every month on a pre-set date. Also, dividends from a share certificate can be automatically transferred to a share draft account. Retired members enjoy this service as it provides regular income.

Telephone Services

Many credit unions offer members the option to conduct transactions and make inquiries over the phone. These services are frequently offered by way of a **voice response unit (VRU)** that allows members to access accounts by pressing buttons on the phone keypad. Members key in an account number or social security number plus personal identification number (PIN) and then make choices among menu options. The most popular uses are to check account balances, review cleared share drafts, and transfer funds between accounts. Members can use this service for a wide range of other options, such as checking rates, re-ordering share drafts, applying for a loan, and stopping payment on a share draft.

Members like the ease of making inquiries and conducting transactions from the comfort and privacy of their home. They also appreciate the 24-hour access these systems provide. If a member gets close to the due date for making a credit card payment, a telephone transfer from a share draft account will be much faster than mailing a draft to the credit union.

Reasons members cite for not using telephone services are a preference for personal service, an inability to verify the numbers they enter by phone, and the lack of a receipt for the transaction. To overcome these objections to using the service, credit unions may offer a menu option of speaking to a member service representative, an automated voice verification of the amount of the transaction, and a reference number on completed transactions. Many members find that once they start using the service and experience its reliability, they become steady users.

> Many credit unions offer members the option to conduct transactions and make inquiries over the phone.

Complete activity 7.1 to find out more about telephone services at your credit union.

ATM and Debit Cards

A service that has become well-established for remote access to accounts is the ATM and/or debit card. The **automated teller machine (ATM)** was introduced first and is a stand-alone computer terminal that allows members to directly make transactions on their accounts by using an access device such as a plastic card that looks like a credit card. The member enters a personal identification number (PIN) to authorize the transaction.

Some ATMs are designed purely as cash dispensers for withdrawals while others can process a variety of transactions. The types of transactions available often include cash withdrawals, deposits, transfers between accounts, and balance inquiries. (Credit unions usually establish a daily limit on cash withdrawals.)

As ATMs have become more sophisticated, other services are being added to the terminals. Examples are printouts of ministatements that show recent transactions on an account, sale of postage stamps, and sale of traveler's checks.

Credit unions are also finding that ATMs can be useful ways to promote services. They may

Member Services

TRANSACTION SYSTEMS

Activity 7.1 What Telephone Services Does Your Credit Union Offer?

1. Does your credit union offer telephone services through a voice response unit?
   _____

2. If it does, what types of transactions and inquiries can a member process? What is most popular?
   _____

3. What benefits do members most value about this service?
   _____

include a brief marketing message, such as "great rates on auto loans," that flashes on the screen until a member inserts an ATM card and starts a transaction. The credit union may also print advertising messages on the transaction receipts or dispense coupons.

To provide widespread access to ATMs, credit unions often own machines and/or participate in ATM networks, such as CIRRUS and PLUS. These networks include machines owned by different financial institutions and private companies that allow a member to at least make withdrawals at any machine. The information about the transaction is electronically transmitted to the credit union, which debits the member's account.

Members may pay fees on ATM cards and transactions. Some credit unions assess a small annual fee for having the card. If a credit union owns an ATM, it does not usually assess fees on transactions. If a member uses an ATM owned by another financial institution or company, a fee, or surcharge may be assessed by the machine owner. However, ATM owners are required to display a sign on the machine or notice on the screen regarding a transaction fee if it will be assessed. Users can cancel a transaction before incurring the fee. To help members avoid ATM fees, credit unions sometimes join together in surcharge-free networks and provide a list of these machines to their members.

ATM transactions are popular services with members. The ATM's capacity to offer members access to their accounts (especially for cash withdrawals) twenty-four hours a day, seven days a week is yet unmatched by most other transaction services.

However, members should be encouraged to maintain good security of their ATM card. Members should keep their PIN and ATM card in separate places.

Members should notify their credit union immediately if their ATM card is stolen, lost, or just can't be located. Credit unions can cancel the card and issue a new one with a different PIN.

At some credit unions, members can obtain a **debit card.** A debit card looks like an ATM card but expands the member's ability to make transactions at other locations, such as retail stores, gas stations, and supermarket chains. When members use their debit cards at these locations, the amount of their purchase is deducted directly from their accounts (usually share draft accounts) and credited to the merchant's account at a financial institution. Members have the benefit of using their share draft account funds without writing out a share draft to the merchant. Some merchants, such as supermarkets, may also allow the member to obtain a certain amount of cash above the purchase amount. The member receives a receipt for the transaction from the merchant.

Some credit unions offer the functions of an ATM card and debit card in the same plastic card. Usually these cards carry the credit union's name plus the Visa or MasterCard logo because the debit card services are processed through these companies (see figure 7.1). The Visa or MasterCard connection also makes these cards acceptable at a huge number of merchants who also accept the credit cards of these companies.

Members value debit cards because they give greater freedom than ATM cards. Members avoid having to carry their checkbook to make purchases. They also do not overextend their credit cards because debit cards deduct the funds directly from the member's account. Members find they can better control their spending this way. Merchants may also be more accepting of debit cards than personal checks due to a lower degree of fraud.

Complete activity 7.2 to expand your knowledge about ATMs and debit cards at your credit union.

Internet-Based Credit Union Services

The Internet is a phenomenon that continues to astonish. The growth continues to surge and credit unions are taking advantage of its opportunities. CUNA/NFO WorldGroup surveys have shown that credit union members are more likely to have personal computers and more likely to use online services than nonmembers. As members use the Internet more, they become more interested in and accepting of Internet-based credit union services. From rudimentary web sites starting in the mid-1990s, credit unions have grown to offer sophisticated sites with a wide range of services (see figure 7.2).

Members value debit cards because they give greater freedom than ATM cards.

Figure 7.1 Sample Debit Card Brochure

> # Visa Check Card
>
> - **Leave your checkbook at home!** Now there's an easier way to pay—with your Dane County Credit Union Visa Check Card.
>
> - **It's easy!** Use your DCCU Visa Check Card to pay for purchases at merchants worldwide who display the Visa logo. The amount of each purchase will be deducted from your checking account. You can use your Check Card at stores, restaurants, to do transactions at ATMs, and to order merchandise by phone or mail.
>
> - **It's convenient!** Carry your DCCU Visa Check Card and you won't have to carry cash or a checkbook. You won't need to take time to write checks, show ID, or wait for a check approval. Plus, every purchase you make with your Check Card is listed on your monthly checking account statement so keeping track of your money is easier, too.
>
> - **It'll save you money!** Once you see how convenient it is to shop with your Visa Check Card, you'll write fewer checks—saving you money in check printing charges. There's no annual fee and when you use the card as a Visa Check Card, there will be no transaction charges.*
>
> - **Apply today!** Any qualified member who has a checking account with Dane County Credit Union may take advantage of our Visa Check Card. Simply complete this application and return it to us.

Source: © Dane County Credit Union, Madison, Wisconsin. Reprinted with permission.

Credit unions that offer a web site may include services in the following three areas: information/advertising, interactive features, and account access and transactions.

Information/Advertising

The Internet is a source of a huge amount of information (and misinformation). Credit unions stay true to their philosophy of "people helping people" by making sure that the information on their web sites is accurate and useful. Part of this information helps members learn more about credit union services and how they can be beneficial. Part of the information helps members be better money managers and shoppers. Examples of web site features that provide information include:

- descriptions of services;
- dividend rate and loan interest rate lists (which are updated as needed);
- information on branch locations, phone numbers, and ATM locations;
- newsletters and articles on money management or smart shopping;
- links to other sites of value to members such as local events, volunteer opportunities, and government sites;
- job openings at the credit union.

Activity 7.2 Expanding Your Knowledge of ATM and Debit Cards

1. Does your credit union own ATMs or participate in an ATM network? Does it offer debit cards?

2. Is the debit card function combined with the ATM card?

3. What limits has the credit union set on withdrawals?

4. Does your credit union charge a fee for these cards or for transactions?

5. How does a member apply for a card?

Credit unions add to this information and keep it up-to-date so that members come back to the site for more.

Interactive Features

Interactive features involve the member with the elements of the site in an active rather than passive way. They take advantage of the power of computers and the communication technology of the Internet. Examples of interactive features include:

- e-mail for communicating between members and staff;
- calculators for "what if" scenarios that apply to retirement planning, savings growth, or loan payments (see figure 7.3);
- member surveys that ask members for reactions or information on a wide variety of topics: Internet services, ease of using the web site, favorite parts of the site, and even fun surveys to promote traffic to the site;
- children's pages to provide games and links to reviewed sites. The children's page may tie in to the credit union's children's club;
- applications for loans or other services. These can be filled out and transmitted to the credit union electronically (see figure 7.4). Response is usually quick when a credit union offers this type of service.

Member Services
TRANSACTION SYSTEMS

Figure 7.2 Sample Credit Union Web Site (Home Page)

Welcome to LANCO Federal Credit Union

| Home Page |
| e-Services |
| Kids |
| Who we are |
| Loans |
| Savings & more |
| Cool Stuff |
| Site Map |
| Newsletter |
| Contact Us |
| Special Events |

Golden Dollar Giveaway
click here to enter

Click Here for
FREE ATM
LOCATIONS

Located at 2024 W. Main St.

Call 717/361/1800 for more information

Click here for this month's newsletter

LANCO Federal Credit Union serves the employees of many Lancaster County educational institutes and businesses. Come in and take a look!

I Who We Are I Loans I Savings & Checking I Cool Stuff I Kids Stuff I Contact Us I

© LANCO Federal Credit Union
Lancaster, Pa.
lanco@lancofcu.com

Source: © LANCO Federal Credit Union, Lancaster, Pennsylvania. Reprinted with permission.

Account Access and Transactions

A credit union's web site can raise the level of service it offers by making it possible for members to securely access their accounts and conduct transactions. This is the most powerful way that web sites help members and credit unions. Account access includes the security of a log-in that requires a PIN or password to access account balances, histories, and conduct transactions.

Types of inquiries and transactions that members may be able to conduct include the following list (see figure 7.5 for examples of various screens that support these services).

- view account balances;
- transfer funds between accounts;
- view scheduled transfers between accounts (such as a loan payment that is automatically transferred from a share draft account);
- view account history to see if share drafts have cleared and on what date;
- issue stop payments;
- reorder checks;
- order copies of share drafts;
- download account histories into personal money management software programs;
- bill payment.

For bill payment, the member can set up a list of regular payees and schedule payments to be made (see figure 7.6 for screens that apply to bill payment). The credit union processes the payments to the payees and the member can check the list of scheduled payments and account history. The payments are made in a similar manner as the automatic bill payments that credit unions have been processing for many years. However, with this new service, members can schedule both recurring payments and one-time payments. Bill payment is considered to be an important service for the future as it retains the member's loyalty to the credit union as the source for trusted transaction processing. The long-term goal is for all bills to be presented electronically as well as paid electronically.

Internet Security

Although delivering financial services by way of Internet access is a growing area, many members have concerns about the security of the information they would transmit and that would be transmitted back to them. They worry that the information could be intercepted on the way and used for fraudulent transactions. Members have a long history of trusting their credit union with their personal financial information because credit unions have a good record of safeguarding it. Credit unions must be committed to carrying this level of security over to online transactions so that member fears can be overcome. As members become more used to online transactions and credit unions are vigilant about security, the level of trust for these transactions is likely to increase.

Member Services

TRANSACTION SYSTEMS

Figure 7.3 Sample Web Site Loan Payment Calculator

LANCO Federal Credit Union

Loan Payment Calculator
If your browser does not support JAVA, or to get an amortization schedule,
use our other calculator.

REQUIRED FIELDS—Enter Interest Rate and Term	
Enter Interest Rate	A.P.R.
Enter Term	Months.
OPTIONAL FIELDS—Complete one of the fields and 'Calculate' the other.	
Amount of loan is:	'Calculate' Loan Amount
Monthly payment is:	'Calculate' Payment Amount

Reset Form

NOTE: This calculator is intended for informational purposes only. It is NOT intended as a disclosure or offer of credit. Your actual payments may vary.

Sidebar navigation:
- Home Page
- e-Services
- Kids
- Who we are
- Loans
  - Loans
  - Loan Rates
  - Loan Calculator
  - Loan Application
  - LANCO VISA
  - Home Loans
- Savings & more
- Cool Stuff
- Site Map
- Newsletter
- Contact Us
- Special Events

I Who We Are I Loans I Savings & Checking I Cool Stuff I Kids Stuff I Contact Us I

© LANCO Federal Credit Union
Lancaster, Pa.
lanco@lancofcu.com

Source: © LANCO Federal Credit Union, Lancaster, Pennsylvania. Reprinted with permission.

Figure 7.4 Sample Web Site Loan Application

LANCO Federal Credit Union
Loan Application

THIS IS A SECURE DOCUMENT

The lock or key at the bottom of your browser should look like one of the above. If it does not, you may have followed an outdated link or used an incorrect URL to access this page. Click Here to reload this page as a secure document.

Please Enter Your Email Address: [ ]

We are only able to process loans for members of LANCO Federal Credit Union. Please call us to see if you are eligible to become a member.

If you are applying for joint credit, secured credit or if you live in a community property state (AZ, CA, ID, LA, NM, NV, TX, WA), please complete the following:
○ Married ○ Separated ○ Unmarried (Single, Divorced, Widowed)

Would you like to purchase Credit Disability Insurance: ○ Yes ○ No

Would you like Payroll Deduction (if available): ○ Yes ○ No

Amount applied for $ [ ] for a period of [ ] months
to be repaid in ○ Weekly ○ Bi-weekly ○ Semi-monthly ○ Monthly payments of $ [ ]

Purpose of the loan: [ ]
Type of loan: ○ *Auto ○ Lease Alternative ○ *Signature ○ Signature Line
○ Shared Secured ○ *Boat/RV ○ Home Equity Line ○ Home Equity Fixed

*Member must keep $100 in primary share account for the term of the loan.

Applicant:	**Joint Applicant:**
Name: [ ]	Name: [ ]
Account #: [ ]	Account #: [ ]
Present Address:	Present Address:
Street: [ ]	Street: [ ]
City: [ ]	City: [ ]
State & Zip: [ ]	State & Zip: [ ]

Source: © LANCO Federal Credit Union, Lancaster, Pennsylvania. Reprinted with permission.

Member Services

TRANSACTION SYSTEMS

Figure 7.4 Sample Web Site Loan Application (Continued)

No. Years: [ ] If less than 2 yrs enter previous address: [ ]	No. Years: [ ] If less than 2 yrs enter previous address: [ ]
Social Security #: [ ] Home Phone #: [ ] Birthdate (MM/DD/YY): [ ]	Social Security #: [ ] Home Phone #: [ ] Birthdate (MM/DD/YY): [ ]
Employer Name/Division: [ ]	Employer Name/Division: [ ]
Employer Address: [ ]	Employer Address: [ ]
Employer Phone #: [ ] Position: [ ] Date Hired (MM/DD/YY): [ ] Yearly Gross $ [ ] Monthly Net $ [ ] Pay Frequency: ○ Weekly ○ Bi=weekly ○ Semi-monthly ○ Monthly Additional Income: $ [ ] per [ ] Complete if current is less than 5 years: Previous Employers Name: [ ] Position: [ ] Yrs Employed: [ ]	Employer Phone #: [ ] Position: [ ] Date Hired (MM/DD/YY): [ ] Yearly Gross $ [ ] Monthly Net $ [ ] Pay Frequency: ○ Weekly ○ Bi=weekly ○ Semi-monthly ○ Monthly Additional Income: $ [ ] per [ ] Complete if current is less than 5 years: Previous Employers Name: [ ] Position: [ ] Yrs Employed: [ ]
Driver's License #: [ ] Nearest Relative Outside of Household: Name: [ ] Address & Phone: [ ]	Driver's License #: [ ] Nearest Relative Outside of Household: Name: [ ] Address & Phone: [ ]
Housing: ○ Own ○ Buying ○ Rent ○ Other Monthly Mortgage/Rent Payment: [ ] Paid To: [ ]	Housing: ○ Own ○ Buying ○ Rent ○ Other Monthly Mortgage/Rent Payment: [ ] Paid To: [ ]

Figure 7.4 Sample Web Site Loan Application (Continued)

LIST ALL DEBTS i.e. CAR LOANS, BANK LOANS, CREDIT CARDS, ETC.
Credit Information—Outstanding Debts

Creditor	Monthly Payment	Balance Owed	Creditor	Monthly Payment	Balance Owed

SECURITY DESCRIPTION (MUST complete if buying or refinancing a car, boat or RV/Trailer)

Year: [ ] Make: [ ] Model: [ ]
Serial Number (MUST have): [ ]
Mileage: [ ]

Price before tax: + [ ]
Taxes: + [ ]
Tags: + [ ]
Cash Down Payment or
Trade-in Allowance: − [ ]
Amount to Finance: = [ ]

Names to be registered on title: [ ]
Accessories: [ ]

Name of Dealer or individual (if buying): [ ]
Salesperson's Name: [ ] Phone Number: [ ]
Financial Institution currently holding title (include Loan #, if refinancing):
[ ]

Figure 7.4 Sample Web Site Loan Application (Continued)

Insurance Information (Required on all vehicle, boat and home loans.)

Name of Company: [   ]
Policy Number & Expiration Date: [   ]
Name of Agent & Phone: [   ]

Asset Information

Type	Description	Amount/Value
Checking Acct		
Savings Acct		
Home		
2nd Home		
Vehicle		
Vehicle		
Other		
Other		

Have you filed bankruptcy in the last 14 years? ○ Yes ○ No
  if yes, what year? [   ] (We will need discharge papers)
Have you ever had auto, furniture or property repossessed? ○ Yes ○ No
Have you ever had credit in any other name? ○ Yes ○ No
  if so, what name? [   ]
Do you have any judgments or lawsuits pending? ○ Yes ○ No
Do you have any past due bills? ○ Yes ○ No
  if so, to whom? [   ] [   ]

You agree that everything stated in this application is correct to the best of your knowledge and that the above information is a completed listing of all your debts and obligations. You authorize the credit union to obtain credit reports and verify any information in connection with this application. If this is a joint application, you are also authorizing the verification of all co-applicant information. You understand that it is a federal crime to wilfully and deliberately provide incomplete or incorrect information on loan applications made to Federal Credit Unions insured by NCUA. If there are any important changes, you will notify us in writing immediately. You also agree to notify us of any change in your name, address or employment within a reasonable time thereafter.

By pressing the "Send Application" button below, you agree to the above statement. You understand that we may require your signature on additional documents prior to disbursing any credit proceeds.

Check here if you are ready to send your application ❑

[Send Request]   [Erase Form]

| Home | Home Banking | Who We Are | Loans | Savings & Checking | Cool Stuff | Kids Stuff | Contact Us |

Member Services

TRANSACTION SYSTEMS

Figure 7.5 Sample Account Access Screens

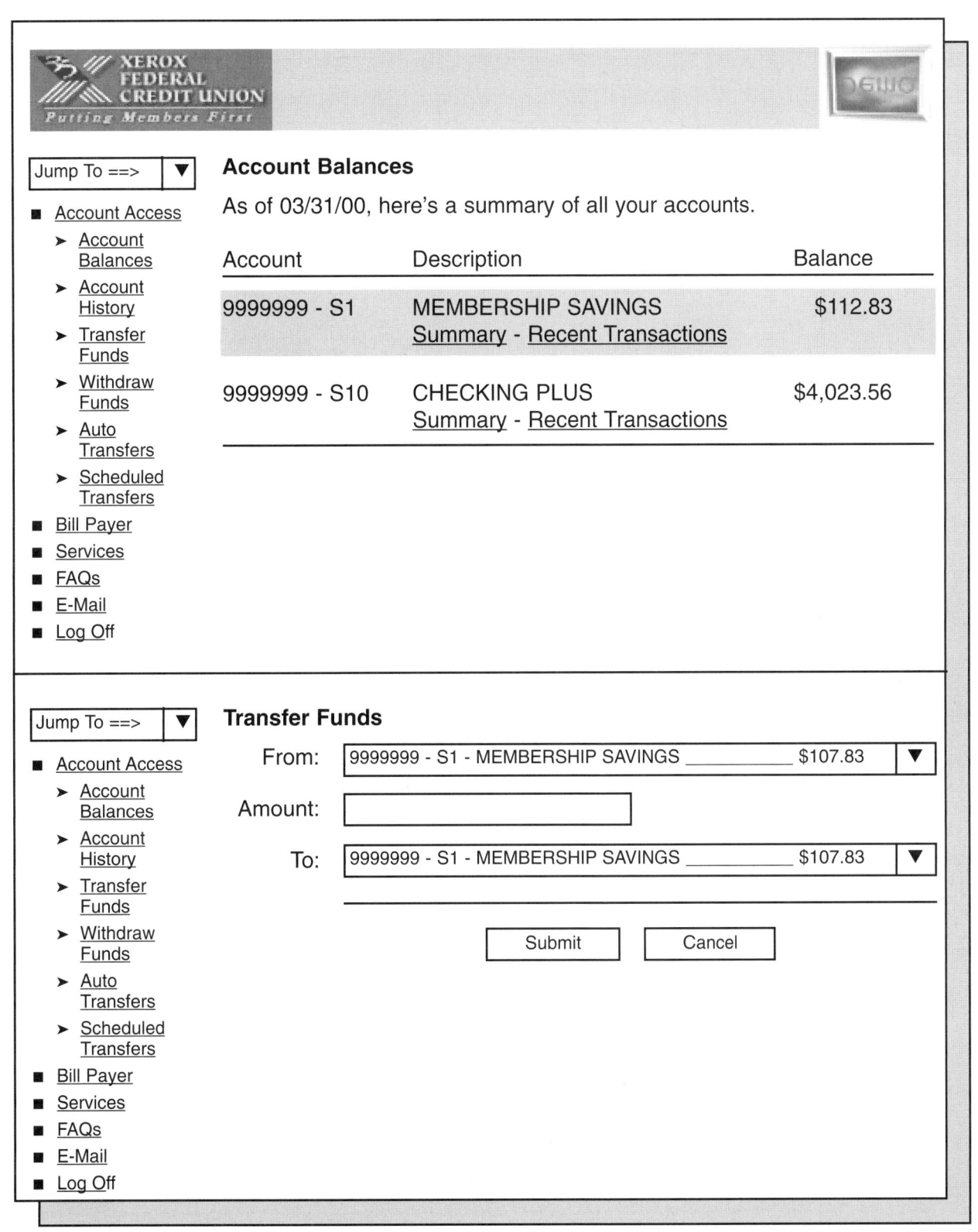

XEROX FEDERAL CREDIT UNION
Putting Members First

Jump To ==> ▼	**Account Balances**
■ Account Access	As of 03/31/00, here's a summary of all your accounts.
➤ Account Balances	
➤ Account History	
➤ Transfer Funds	
➤ Withdraw Funds	
➤ Auto Transfers	
➤ Scheduled Transfers	
■ Bill Payer	
■ Services	
■ FAQs	
■ E-Mail	
■ Log Off	

Account	Description	Balance
9999999 - S1	MEMBERSHIP SAVINGS Summary - Recent Transactions	$112.83
9999999 - S10	CHECKING PLUS Summary - Recent Transactions	$4,023.56

Jump To ==> ▼	**Transfer Funds**
■ Account Access	From: [9999999 - S1 - MEMBERSHIP SAVINGS $107.83 ▼]
➤ Account Balances	Amount: [ ]
➤ Account History	To: [9999999 - S1 - MEMBERSHIP SAVINGS $107.83 ▼]
➤ Transfer Funds	
➤ Withdraw Funds	[Submit] [Cancel]
➤ Auto Transfers	
➤ Scheduled Transfers	
■ Bill Payer	
■ Services	
■ FAQs	
■ E-Mail	
■ Log Off	

Source: © Xerox Federal Credit Union, El Segundo, California. Reprinted with permission.

Member Services

TRANSACTION SYSTEMS

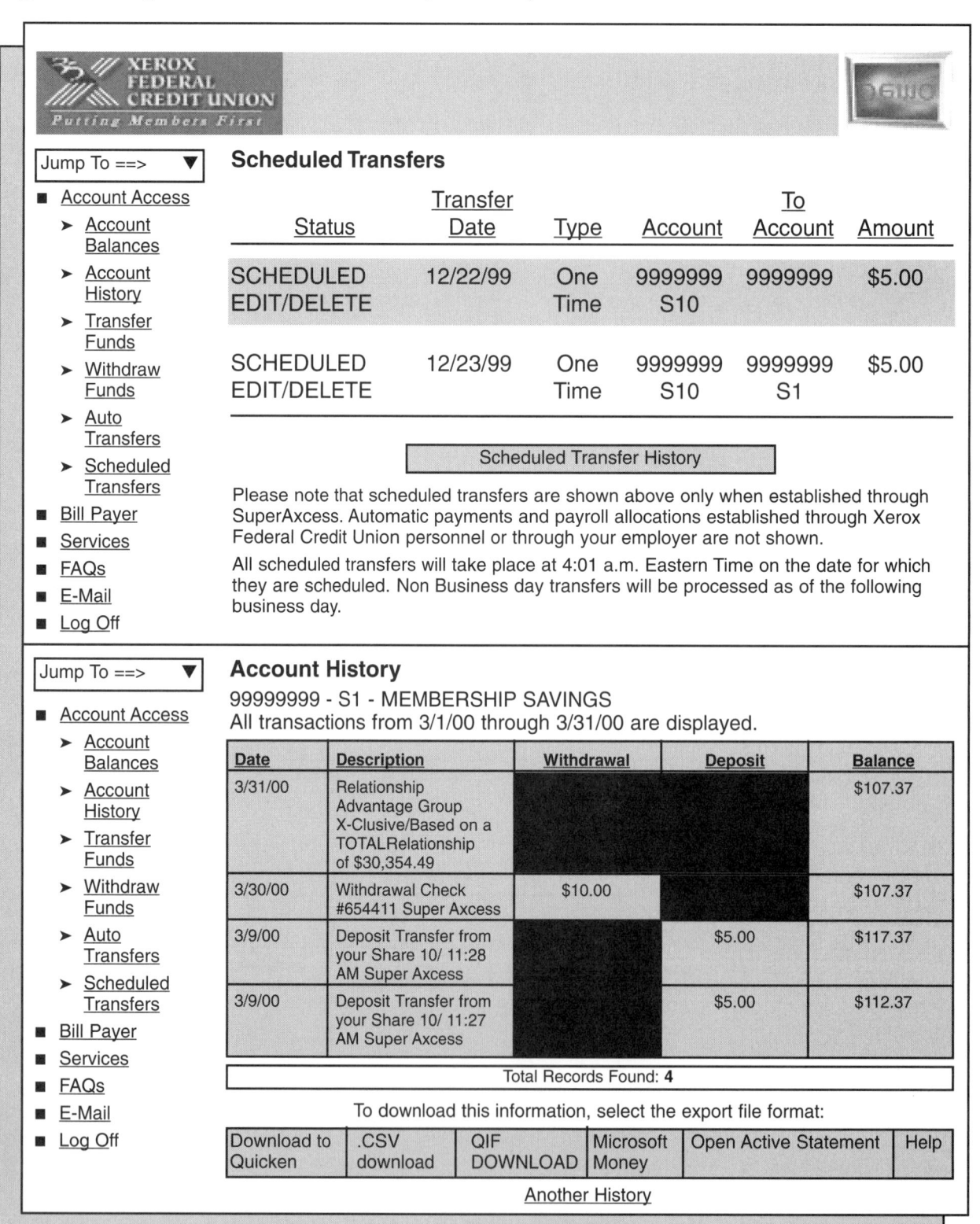

Figure 7.5 Sample Account Access Screens (Continued)

XEROX FEDERAL CREDIT UNION
Putting Members First

Jump To ==> ▼
- Account Access
  - ➤ Account Balances
  - ➤ Account History
  - ➤ Transfer Funds
  - ➤ Withdraw Funds
  - ➤ Auto Transfers
  - ➤ Scheduled Transfers
- Bill Payer
- Services
- FAQs
- E-Mail
- Log Off

Scheduled Transfers

Status	Transfer Date	Type	Account	To Account	Amount
SCHEDULED EDIT/DELETE	12/22/99	One Time	9999999 S10	9999999	$5.00
SCHEDULED EDIT/DELETE	12/23/99	One Time	9999999 S10	9999999 S1	$5.00

Scheduled Transfer History

Please note that scheduled transfers are shown above only when established through SuperAxcess. Automatic payments and payroll allocations established through Xerox Federal Credit Union personnel or through your employer are not shown.

All scheduled transfers will take place at 4:01 a.m. Eastern Time on the date for which they are scheduled. Non Business day transfers will be processed as of the following business day.

Jump To ==> ▼
- Account Access
  - ➤ Account Balances
  - ➤ Account History
  - ➤ Transfer Funds
  - ➤ Withdraw Funds
  - ➤ Auto Transfers
  - ➤ Scheduled Transfers
- Bill Payer
- Services
- FAQs
- E-Mail
- Log Off

Account History
99999999 - S1 - MEMBERSHIP SAVINGS
All transactions from 3/1/00 through 3/31/00 are displayed.

Date	Description	Withdrawal	Deposit	Balance
3/31/00	Relationship Advantage Group X-Clusive/Based on a TOTALRelationship of $30,354.49			$107.37
3/30/00	Withdrawal Check #654411 Super Axcess	$10.00		$107.37
3/9/00	Deposit Transfer from your Share 10/ 11:28 AM Super Axcess		$5.00	$117.37
3/9/00	Deposit Transfer from your Share 10/ 11:27 AM Super Axcess		$5.00	$112.37

Total Records Found: 4

To download this information, select the export file format:

| Download to Quicken | .CSV download | QIF DOWNLOAD | Microsoft Money | Open Active Statement | Help |

Another History

118

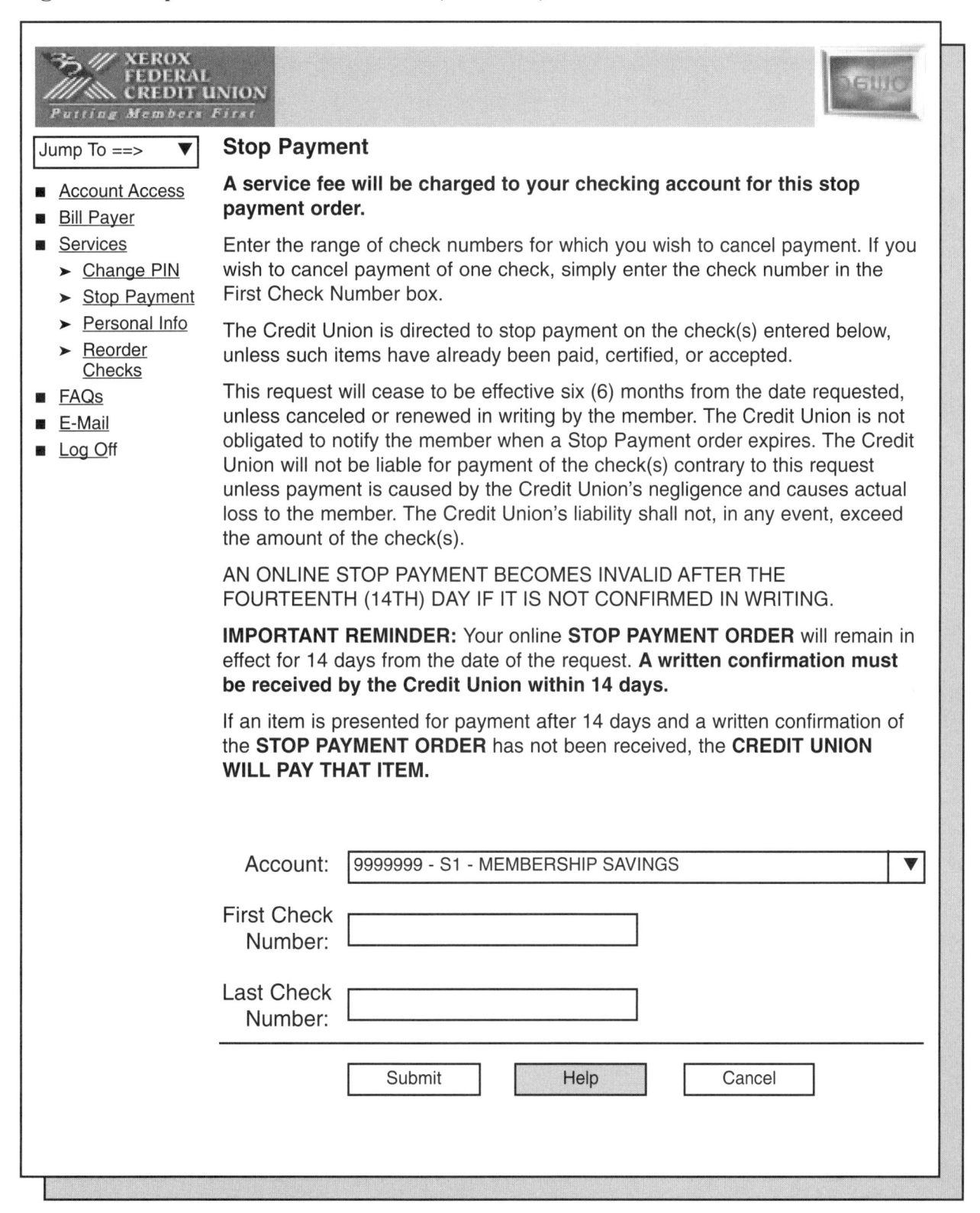

Figure 7.5 Sample Account Access Screens (Continued)

XEROX FEDERAL CREDIT UNION
Putting Members First

Jump To ==> ▼

- Account Access
- Bill Payer
- Services
  ➤ Change PIN
  ➤ Stop Payment
  ➤ Personal Info
  ➤ Reorder Checks
- FAQs
- E-Mail
- Log Off

Stop Payment

A service fee will be charged to your checking account for this stop payment order.

Enter the range of check numbers for which you wish to cancel payment. If you wish to cancel payment of one check, simply enter the check number in the First Check Number box.

The Credit Union is directed to stop payment on the check(s) entered below, unless such items have already been paid, certified, or accepted.

This request will cease to be effective six (6) months from the date requested, unless canceled or renewed in writing by the member. The Credit Union is not obligated to notify the member when a Stop Payment order expires. The Credit Union will not be liable for payment of the check(s) contrary to this request unless payment is caused by the Credit Union's negligence and causes actual loss to the member. The Credit Union's liability shall not, in any event, exceed the amount of the check(s).

AN ONLINE STOP PAYMENT BECOMES INVALID AFTER THE FOURTEENTH (14TH) DAY IF IT IS NOT CONFIRMED IN WRITING.

IMPORTANT REMINDER: Your online **STOP PAYMENT ORDER** will remain in effect for 14 days from the date of the request. **A written confirmation must be received by the Credit Union within 14 days.**

If an item is presented for payment after 14 days and a written confirmation of the **STOP PAYMENT ORDER** has not been received, the **CREDIT UNION WILL PAY THAT ITEM.**

Account: | 9999999 - S1 - MEMBERSHIP SAVINGS | ▼ |

First Check Number: [   ]

Last Check Number: [   ]

[Submit] [Help] [Cancel]

Member Services

TRANSACTION SYSTEMS

Figure 7.5 Sample Account Access Screens (Continued)

XEROX FEDERAL CREDIT UNION
Putting Members First

Jump To ==> ▼

- Account Access
- Bill Payer
- Services
  ➤ Change PIN
  ➤ Stop Payment
  ➤ Personal Info
  ➤ Reorder Checks
- FAQs
- E-Mail
- Log Off

Reorder Checks

Account Number:	9999999 - S10 - REGULAR CHECKING
Name(s) that should appear on the checks:	JOHN SMITH
Address:	111 MAIN STREET
City:	ANYTOWN
State:	XX
Zip:	00000
Daytime Phone Number:	(555) 555-5555

If you would like your Telephone Number and/or Drivers License Number printed on your checks enter the information here:

Telephone Number:

Drivers License Number:

Check Style:

Please check the XFCU web site for the various check styles

150 Duplicate Checks and 30 Deposit Slips

XFCU Custom Image ▼

Starting Check Number (101 to 9000):

Number of Boxes: ○ One   ○ Two   ○ Three

Special Instructions:

Submit   Cancel

120

Member Services
TRANSACTION SYSTEMS

Figure 7.6 Sample Bill Payment Screens

XEROX FEDERAL CREDIT UNION
Putting Members First

Jump To ==> ▼	**Add a Payee**

- Account Access
- Bill Payer
  - **Scheduled Payments**
  - Payment History
  - Make a Payment
  - Add a Payee
  - Payee Maintenance
- Services
- FAQs
- E-Mail
- Log Off

Payee Information:

Payee Name: [   ]
Address 1: [   ]
Address 2: [   ]
City: [   ] State: [ ] Zip: [   ]
Phone: [   ]
Payee Account: [   ]

Payment Information:

Debit Account: [99999999 - S10- REGULAR CHECKING ▼]

Recurring Payments

☐ Click here to make this a Recurring Payee

[Submit]   [Cancel]

For Bill Payer concerns, please call Metavante at 1-800-825-4321. Please have your Bill Pay ID ready when you call. Your Bill Pay ID is 0000000.

Source: © Xerox Federal Credit Union, El Segundo, California. Reprinted with permission.

Member Services

TRANSACTION SYSTEMS

Figure 7.6 Sample Bill Payment Screens (Continued)

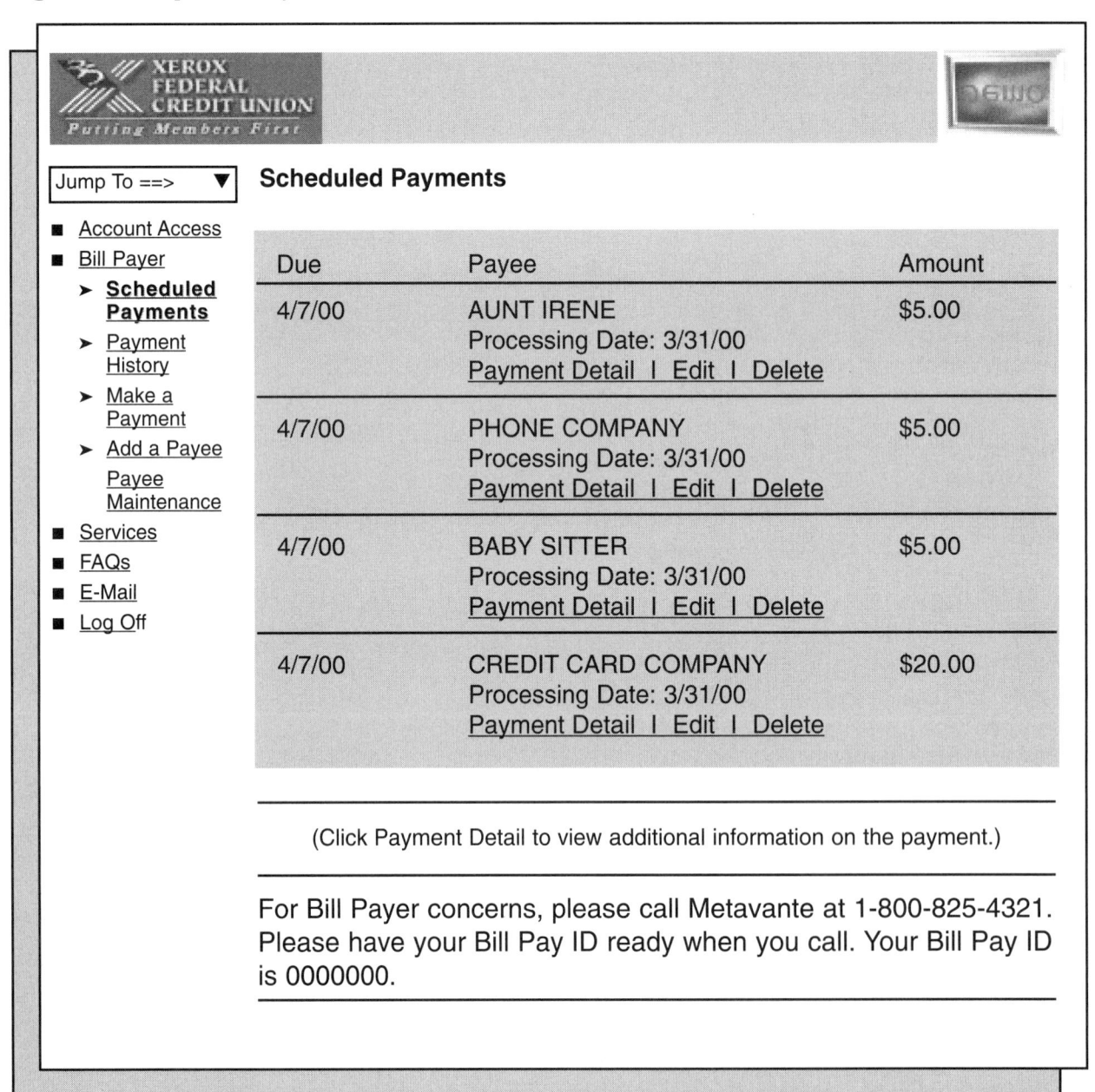

XEROX FEDERAL CREDIT UNION
Putting Members First

Jump To ==> ▼

- Account Access
- Bill Payer
  ➤ **Scheduled Payments**
  ➤ Payment History
  ➤ Make a Payment
  ➤ Add a Payee
  Payee Maintenance
- Services
- FAQs
- E-Mail
- Log Off

Scheduled Payments

Due	Payee	Amount
4/7/00	AUNT IRENE Processing Date: 3/31/00 Payment Detail I Edit I Delete	$5.00
4/7/00	PHONE COMPANY Processing Date: 3/31/00 Payment Detail I Edit I Delete	$5.00
4/7/00	BABY SITTER Processing Date: 3/31/00 Payment Detail I Edit I Delete	$5.00
4/7/00	CREDIT CARD COMPANY Processing Date: 3/31/00 Payment Detail I Edit I Delete	$20.00

(Click Payment Detail to view additional information on the payment.)

For Bill Payer concerns, please call Metavante at 1-800-825-4321. Please have your Bill Pay ID ready when you call. Your Bill Pay ID is 0000000.

Member Benefits of Internet Credit Union Services

Members who use these services enjoy the convenience and "anytime" access. Members who sign up for online transaction services may have already found automatic transfers, ATM/debit cards, and telephone services to be useful in saving them time and travel when using credit union services. These members have found technology to be helpful in making their lives easier.

Figure 7.6 Sample Bill Payment Screens (Continued)

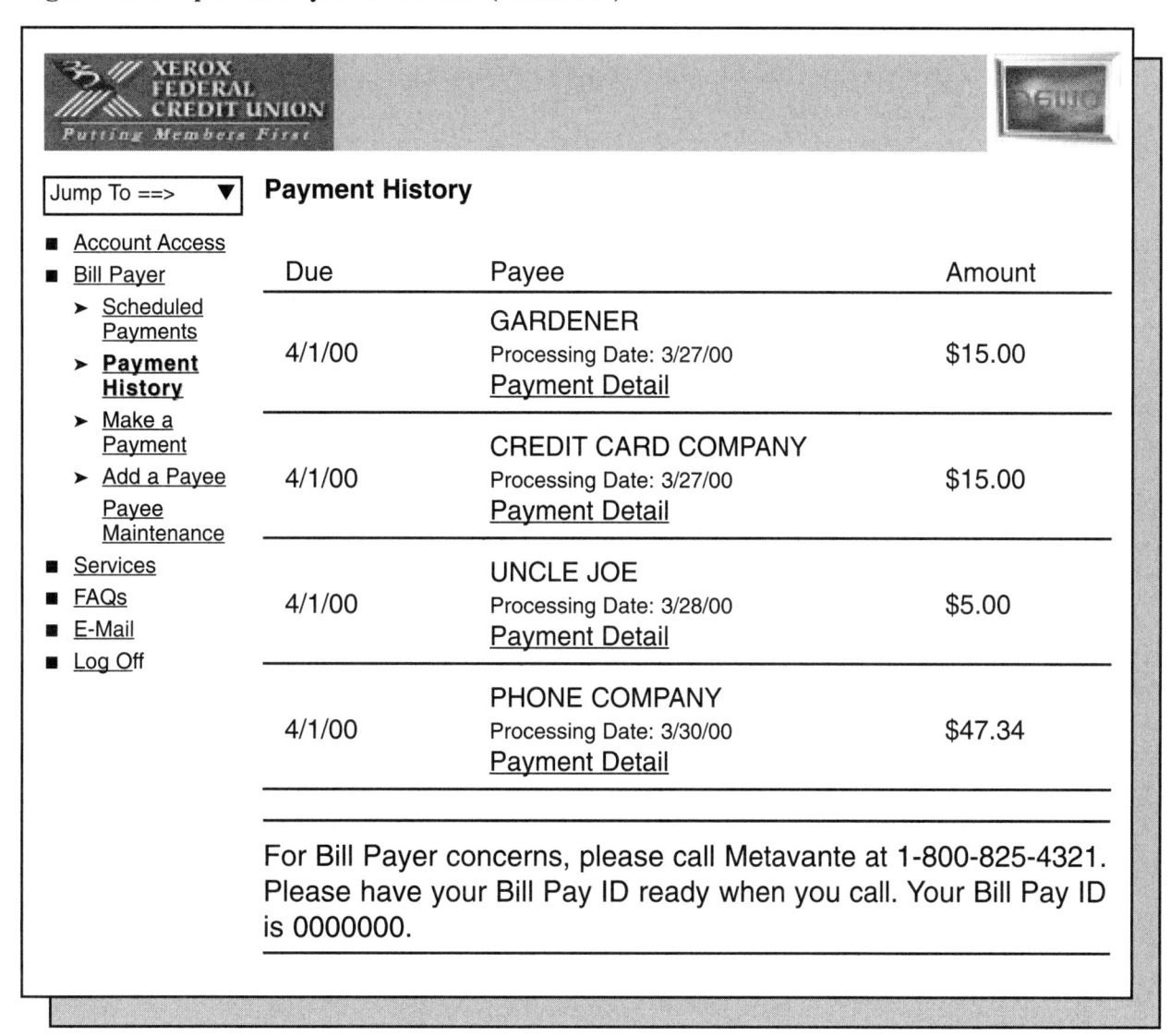

XEROX FEDERAL CREDIT UNION
Putting Members First

Jump To ==> ▼

- Account Access
- Bill Payer
  ➤ Scheduled Payments
  ➤ **Payment History**
  ➤ Make a Payment
  ➤ Add a Payee
     Payee Maintenance
- Services
- FAQs
- E-Mail
- Log Off

Payment History

Due	Payee	Amount
4/1/00	GARDENER Processing Date: 3/27/00 Payment Detail	$15.00
4/1/00	CREDIT CARD COMPANY Processing Date: 3/27/00 Payment Detail	$15.00
4/1/00	UNCLE JOE Processing Date: 3/28/00 Payment Detail	$5.00
4/1/00	PHONE COMPANY Processing Date: 3/30/00 Payment Detail	$47.34

For Bill Payer concerns, please call Metavante at 1-800-825-4321. Please have your Bill Pay ID ready when you call. Your Bill Pay ID is 0000000.

Internet-based services may simply be an extension and improvement to these other systems. Internet-based services allow a member to use a broader range of services than telephone services—although at times a quick phone call is the fastest way to check a balance or make a transfer. Internet-based services can offer services that may not be available by way of an ATM/debit card, but they have yet to furnish the ability to get cash!

Members are finding that they need to develop a broader view of how they use credit union services. In today's financial environment, members need to find the combination of transaction systems that best meets their needs.

Transaction Systems and Personal Service

Credit unions provide a variety of transaction systems but they also continually recognize that members still value personal service. Members want the comfort of knowing that the credit union still has an office with human beings who can answer their questions and solve their problems. Members may like quickly getting cash at an ATM or having their payroll automatically deposited but these transactions are the ones that many members consider routine.

While some members quickly embrace these new technologies, others are not comfortable and need guidance and reassurance when using them. The conflicting technology orientation of members is reflected in a CUNA/NFO WorldGroup survey that found 56 percent of primary credit union members agreed that "technology has improved the quality of my life." In contrast, 37 percent said that the "variety of ways to conduct banking today is confusing." Members may be concerned about accuracy of transactions when using these new transaction systems. If so, they need explanations of security measures and the strong consumer protection laws on electronic transactions. (See STAR module, *S610 Working with Technology,* for more information on how policies, procedures, and laws protect members against losses from unauthorized transactions.)

Above all else, when members need your help, they appreciate that the credit union staff will always be there for them.

Complete activity 7.3 to explore ways to reassure members about using newer transaction systems.

Credit unions provide a variety of transaction systems but they also continually recognize that members still value personal service.

Member Services

TRANSACTION SYSTEMS

Activity 7.3 Working with Members and New Transaction Systems

1. Why do you think so many members say that technology has improved their lives? What benefits do you see from new transaction systems?

   _____
   _____
   _____

2. Why do you think many members have said that the variety of ways to conduct banking is confusing?

   _____
   _____
   _____

3. How can you reassure members that new transaction systems are reliable and worth trying?

   _____
   _____
   _____

Chapter 8 Other Services

Credit unions have a variety of additional member services beyond savings accounts, share accounts, loans, and other transaction services. These services enrich the financial help that a member can obtain from a credit union. This chapter covers the following types of additional services:

- check services
- safe deposit boxes
- notary service
- financial education services
- insurance services
- financial planning services
- investment services

Check Services

Credit unions offer share draft services that primarily cover the everyday needs of credit union members. In addition, credit unions can offer other check services.

Money Orders

Offered for sale in most credit unions, money orders are considered the same as cash because they are guaranteed by the issuer (see figure 8.1). Members often purchase money orders if they do not have a share draft account and need to send payments by mail, or if a creditor requires that payment cannot be made by personal check or share draft.

A money order is like a certified check in that it guarantees payment when properly filled out and endorsed. However, while a certified check is drawn on a member's savings account, and a bank or credit union official attests the funds to cover it have been set aside, a money order needs no guarantee, because the purchase price covers payment.

The Postal Service, banks, credit unions, and even retail stores sell money orders. Most

Objectives

> **Upon completion of this chapter, you will be able to**
> 1. **describe features of money orders and traveler's checks;**
> 2. **explain what types of items should and should not be kept in safe deposit boxes;**
> 3. **list types of financial education services that credit unions provide to members;**
> 4. **list and explain types of insurance available to members;**
> 5. **differentiate term and whole life insurance;**
> 6. **describe types of financial planning and investment services available to members.**

Member Services

OTHER SERVICES

Figure 8.1 Sample Money Order

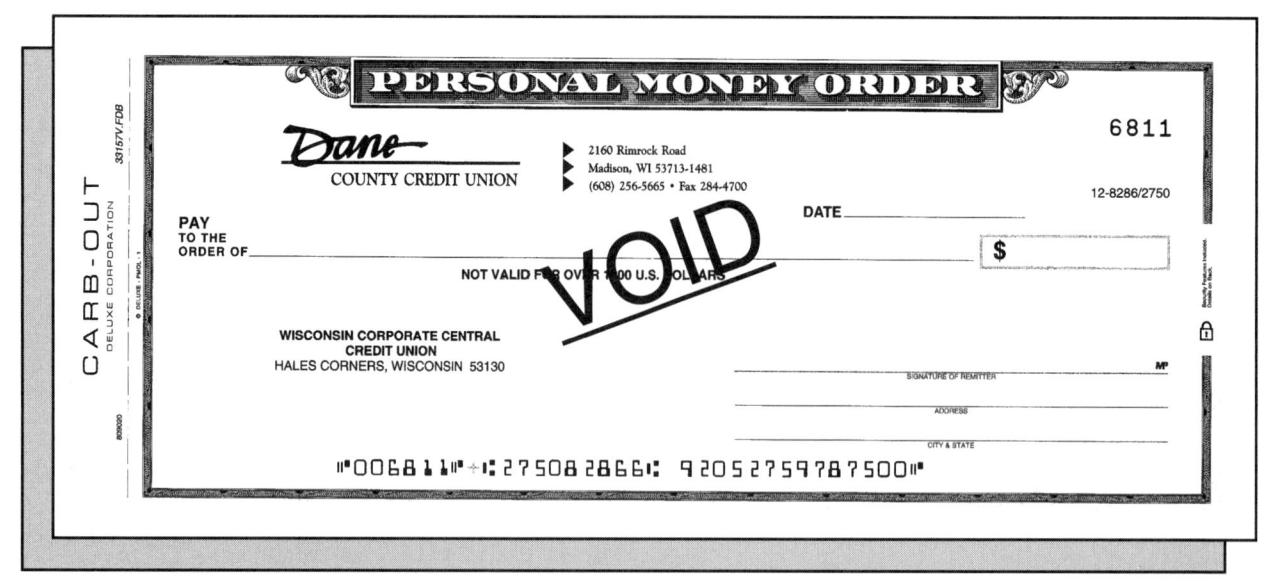

Source: © Dane County Credit Union, Madison, Wisconsin. Reprinted with permission.

institutions issuing money orders limit the amount for which they can be written. Some commercial money orders may show limits as high as $1,000, while a postal money order cannot exceed $700. Usually a small fee is charged for the purchase of money orders.

Traveler's Checks

More and more credit unions offer their members traveler's checks. Like money orders, these checks are considered the same as cash and are guaranteed in the event they are lost or stolen. Credit unions obtain travelers checks from any one of a number of companies (such as VISA or American Express) and offer them to members for a minimal charge (see figure 8.2). Financial institutions, express companies, and even travel agencies usually issue them in denominations up to $500.

When purchasing traveler's checks, the member usually signs them in the presence of a credit union employee. When the checks are cashed, they must be countersigned (signed again on a different line). Traveler's checks are acceptable almost everywhere in the world.

Complete activity 8.1 to learn about check services at your credit union.

Safe Deposit Boxes

Safe deposit boxes provide a means for members to secure valuables or family heirlooms against fire, theft, or damage.

These boxes are located in the credit union's vault or another highly secured area. High-tech security systems guard them and some are even climate controlled. Members usually rent boxes on an annual basis, and the charges vary, depending upon the size of the deposit box.

Encourage members to keep their valuables in a safe deposit box. Items such as birth and marriage certificates, military service papers, citizenship papers, medals, stamps, deeds, trust agreements, contracts, leases, court decrees, and securities are commonly stored in safe deposit boxes.

While members should be encouraged to deposit their valuables in a secured container at your credit union, they should also be advised of what *not* to store in safe deposit boxes. Documents that will be needed immediately when a member dies should not be kept in such boxes. When the owner of a safe deposit box dies, the box is normally sealed until legal procedures have been completed to allow someone to access the contents. As a rule, advise members not to store the following items in these boxes:

- **Wills.** An original will should be kept at the member's home, or in the vault of an attorney, executor, or accountant. Cemetery deeds and burial instructions should also be kept out of the box in order to prevent them from being inaccessible when they are needed.

- **Large amounts of cash.** Keeping large sums of cash in a safe deposit box could be construed as an indication of some sort of criminal activity or as an intent to evade income taxes.

- **Unregistered property belonging to others.** Such items as jewelry or bearer bonds that belong to someone else may be presumed to be the property of the safe deposit box owner. In the event of the box owner's death, the estate or the property owner would have to prove such items did not belong to the box owner, which could be difficult or impossible to do. Otherwise, the items would be included in the decedent's estate and distributed to heirs.

Notary Service

A frequently used service credit unions offer is that of a notary public. Many credit unions have at least one staff person authorized to notarize official documents. A notary certifies signatures and documents for authenticity. Sometimes a small fee is charged for this service.

While members should be encouraged to deposit their valuables in a secured container at your credit union, they should also be advised of what *not* to store in safe deposit boxes.

Figure 8.2 Sample Traveler's Check

Source: © Visa International Service Association.

Financial Education Services

Part of a credit union's mission is to help members be smart about how they manage and use their money. To fulfill this mission, many credit unions offer no-cost seminars on budgeting, car buying, shopping for and financing a home, retirement planning, financing an education, estate planning, using credit wisely, surviving a layoff, and other topics. Some credit unions offer members the use of a library of pamphlets, books, and videos on financial topics. Some credit unions assist members by providing debt counseling when a member is having trouble meeting his or her obligations.

Complete activity 8.2 to find out more about the financial education services your credit union offers.

Insurance Services

As described in earlier chapters, many credit unions offer life savings insurance, credit life insurance, and credit disability insurance. In addition, credit unions may offer other types of insurance, usually through a credit union service organization (CUSO).

Accidental death and dismemberment (AD&D) insurance is a savings and loan protection plan that provides protection for the credit union and the members' surviving families against the hardship of

Activity 8.1 Checking on Checks

1. What is the maximum amount available on money orders sold at your credit union?

2. What fee does your credit union charge to purchase a money order?

3. What does a member do if he or she loses a money order?

4. Does your credit union sell traveler's checks? If so, what brand?

5. What fee does your credit union charge on traveler's checks?

6. What does a member do if he or she loses a traveler's check?

---

outstanding debt. The credit union may provide the coverage free of charge or at a small fee. Members can often purchase an additional amount of coverage if they wish.

Members may also have access to other types of insurance such as auto, home, health, disability, long-term care, and life. Credit unions offer a variety of financial protection plans against liabilities arising from accidents with vehicles, such as autos, vans, and trucks. In addition, many types of insurance coverage are available for homeowners. Coverage and costs vary, but the intent is to provide protection for personal property, liability for actions resulting in losses to others in connection with the property (whether auto or home), or in case of death.

Health, disability, and long-term care insurance recognize that illness and injury can have devastating effects on a family's finances as well as overall quality of life. Members are likely to sign up for these plans if their employers do not offer them or supplemental coverage is desired. These plans pay at least part of health care expenses or compensate for loss of income due to a disability.

Two types of life insurance are common: whole life and term life.

OTHER SERVICES

Whole life insurance is intended to provide coverage over the member's whole life. Whole life insurance accumulates a cash value that increases the longer the policy is held. This gives the member a savings feature to the insurance. The member can borrow against the cash value of a whole life policy. If the loan is still outstanding when the member dies, some or all of the insurance funds go to pay off the loan. If the member pays off the loan before death, the full amount of the insurance coverage is restored. Or, if the member decides to cancel the insurance, he or she would receive a payout based on the cash value.

Term life insurance is a life insurance plan that provides protection for a set period of time, such as five, ten or twenty years. Term life has no cash value and usually has a lower premium than whole life. Many people find that they need substantial life insurance during certain periods of their life, such as while children are growing up and then going on to higher education. If a member dies while his or her children are young, the member would want the family to have sufficient funds while the children grew up. However, after the children are grown, the member does not need as much insurance and the term insurance would end. It is not unusual for members to have term life insurance in addition to whole life insurance so that they have high coverage for part of their lives and a lower level in later years.

Other types of life insurance plans are available and can include investment components.

Familiarize yourself with the variety of insurance plans available at your credit union so that you can direct members to the appropriate specialists. A combination of these insurance services provides a balanced package of protection against loss of income, health care expenses, property losses, liability costs, and survivors' needs.

Financial Planning Services

Over the years, credit unions have come to see that many members need a broader financial plan than simply picking and choosing from credit union services on their own. A CUNA/NFO WorldGroup survey showed that 48 percent of credit union members agreed that "too much information makes financial decisions difficult." In the same survey, 60 percent of members said they needed some type of financial advice.

To meet members' needs, some credit unions offer financial planning services (through an outside organization or CUSO). Members can meet with a financial advisor to assess their needs. The services often include workbooks (including online versions) for assessing members' financial situations. Members can

---

Part of a credit union's mission is to help members be smart about how they manage and use their money.

Activity 8.2 How Does Your Credit Union Offer Financial Education to Members?

Find out what types of services your credit union offers that helps members better manage their money. Are seminars offered? Publications? Debt counseling? Others?

_____
_____
_____
_____
_____

use formulas or online financial calculators to work through various "what-if" scenarios for estimating retirement income, savings accumulation results, and others. After putting this all together, the members and financial advisor can develop a long-term plan for insurance needs, investments, and wise use of debt. Financial planning services may also offer other sources of help such as newsletters and seminars.

Investment Services

As part of financial planning, members may decide that they are interested in types of investments in addition to credit union savings accounts and share certificates. Credit unions that offer financial planning services also usually provide securities brokerage services through a securities broker/dealer associated with the credit union (see figure 8.3).

These broker/dealers provide a wide range of products such as stocks, bonds, mutual funds, annuities, and life insurance. (Many of these investments can be used for a member's IRA savings, also.) A **stock** share is a direct ownership interest in a company. A **bond** is a long-term debt instrument that pays interest and is issued by a business, government, or government agency. A **mutual fund** is a type of investment company that makes diversified investments according to stated investment objectives and by pooling funds from a large number of investors. A professional money manager manages an individual fund and directs the investments. Investors buy shares directly from the mutual fund and sell them back when they want to redeem them. Investors appreciate the advantage of investing in dozens or even hundreds of companies and spreading the risk and return potential. A wide range of funds with different investment

Member Services
OTHER SERVICES

> Many members need a broader financial plan than simply picking and choosing from credit union services on their own.

objectives are available. An **annuity** is offered by an insurance company and is a fixed or variable investment that makes regular payments to the member upon maturity.

It is important that members know that investment products such as these are not insured by the National Credit Union Share Insurance Fund (NCUSIF), not guaranteed by the credit union, and involve investment risks, including possible loss of principal. Credit union members who ask employees about these types of investments should be referred to the appropriate investment representatives.

To learn more about investments available to credit union members, see the STAR module, *S820 Investment Choices for Members*.

Complete activity 8.3 to complete your study of your credit union's services.

Looking to the Future

Looking back over what you have learned in this module, we hope you are impressed with the variety and number of credit union services that members have available. By working through the activities in this module, you have expanded your knowledge of your own credit union's services.

More services and variations on existing ones will continue to be added to this rich tapestry of financial services. Examples that are not yet widely used but may become so include:

- **Smart, or stored value, cards.** These plastic cards contain an imbedded computer microchip. The chip can hold information and an electronic fund of "money." Individuals can recharge these stored value cards and use them like ATM or debit cards. However, these cards can hold additional information that speeds up transactions, opens security doors, identifies the holder, and can even tell you which library books you have checked out.

- **New identification systems.** To improve security for ATM cards and other transaction systems, people are using other methods of identification, such as identifying a member from a fingertip scan. Machines that scan the iris of the eye for identification are also being used.

- **New ways to process checks and share drafts.** Decades ago, futurists predicted a "checkless society." However, consumers and businesses continue to use a large volume of checks so this state has yet to be achieved. Therefore, financial institutions find new ways to clear checks and share drafts faster and more efficiently. One system can electronically capture the information on a check or

Figure 8.3 Sample Financial Planning and Investment Services

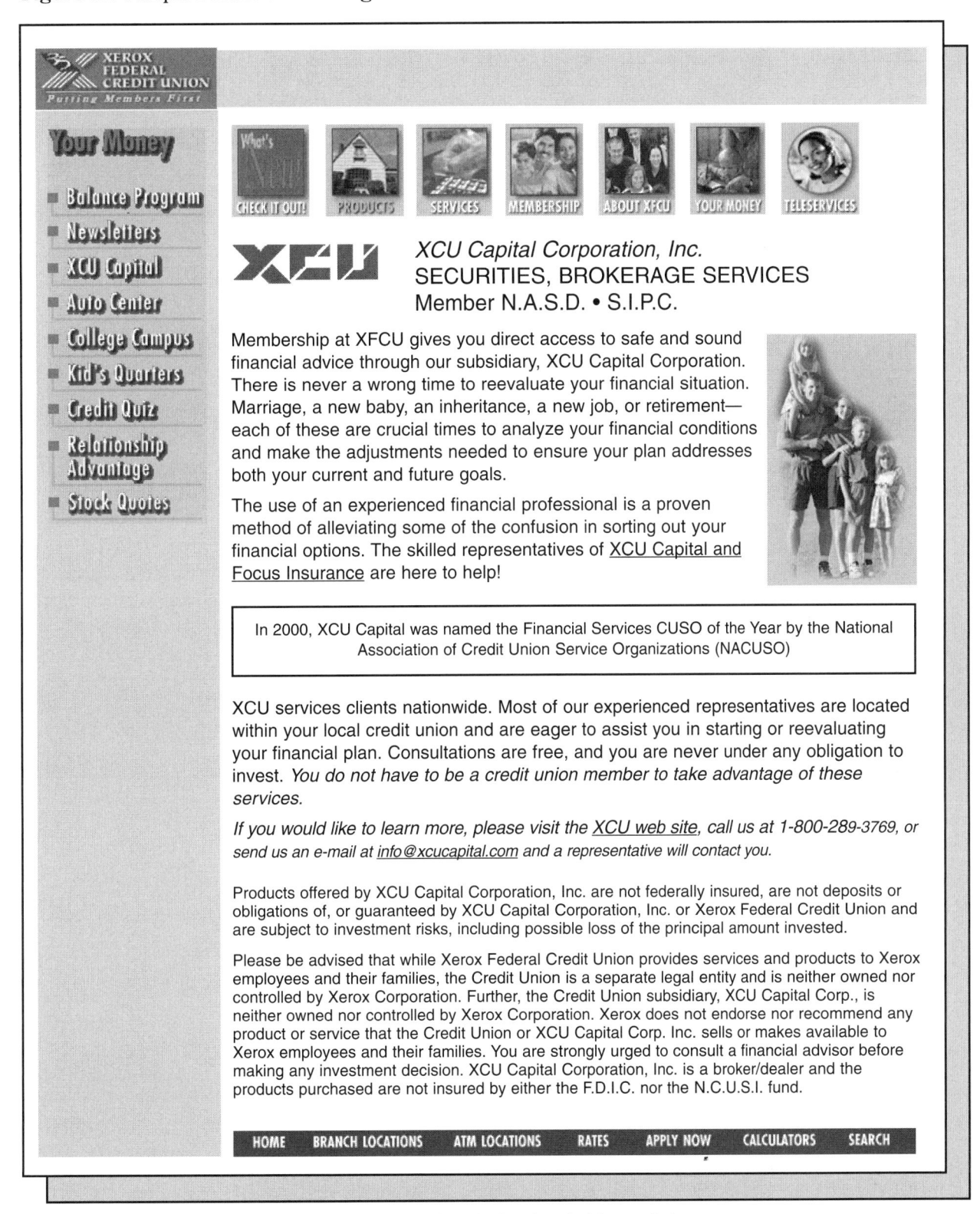

XCU Capital Corporation, Inc.
SECURITIES, BROKERAGE SERVICES
Member N.A.S.D. • S.I.P.C.

Membership at XFCU gives you direct access to safe and sound financial advice through our subsidiary, XCU Capital Corporation. There is never a wrong time to reevaluate your financial situation. Marriage, a new baby, an inheritance, a new job, or retirement—each of these are crucial times to analyze your financial conditions and make the adjustments needed to ensure your plan addresses both your current and future goals.

The use of an experienced financial professional is a proven method of alleviating some of the confusion in sorting out your financial options. The skilled representatives of XCU Capital and Focus Insurance are here to help!

In 2000, XCU Capital was named the Financial Services CUSO of the Year by the National Association of Credit Union Service Organizations (NACUSO)

XCU services clients nationwide. Most of our experienced representatives are located within your local credit union and are eager to assist you in starting or reevaluating your financial plan. Consultations are free, and you are never under any obligation to invest. *You do not have to be a credit union member to take advantage of these services.*

If you would like to learn more, please visit the XCU web site, call us at 1-800-289-3769, or send us an e-mail at info@xcucapital.com and a representative will contact you.

Products offered by XCU Capital Corporation, Inc. are not federally insured, are not deposits or obligations of, or guaranteed by XCU Capital Corporation, Inc. or Xerox Federal Credit Union and are subject to investment risks, including possible loss of the principal amount invested.

Please be advised that while Xerox Federal Credit Union provides services and products to Xerox employees and their families, the Credit Union is a separate legal entity and is neither owned nor controlled by Xerox Corporation. Further, the Credit Union subsidiary, XCU Capital Corp., is neither owned nor controlled by Xerox Corporation. Xerox does not endorse nor recommend any product or service that the Credit Union or XCU Capital Corp. Inc. sells or makes available to Xerox employees and their families. You are strongly urged to consult a financial advisor before making any investment decision. XCU Capital Corporation, Inc. is a broker/dealer and the products purchased are not insured by either the F.D.I.C. nor the N.C.U.S.I. fund.

Source: © Xerox Federal Credit Union, El Segundo, California. Reprinted with permission.

Member Services

OTHER SERVICES

Activity 8.3 What Other Services Does Your Credit Union Offer?

Look back over the topics and services covered in the chapters in this module. Are there any other services your credit union offers that were not covered in this module? If so, list them below and write down the person or department that handles them.

Credit Union Service	Person or Department that Handles this Service

share draft. In the future, a merchant who accepts a check could use a scanner to "read" the information on the check and then use the electronic record to process the payment rather than having the check laboriously travel through the clearing system.

- **More online services.** As personal computers become more widespread, more financial transactions will be processed using online systems, whether the member uses a computer at home, work, or at a credit union office. ATMs are also offering a greater variety of services and may be used to access a credit union's web site. Members will have easy access to bill payment systems that reduce the drudgery of manual bill payment.

Member Services
OTHER SERVICES

Many services that were simply intriguing ideas years ago are turning into realities today. By staying alert to these new services, and continuing to develop your knowledge, you will be prepared for the changes that will continue to improve credit union operations and member services.

> Many services that were simply intriguing ideas years ago are turning into realities today.

Appendix A Answers to Activities

Activity 1.1 Analyzing Members' Financial Needs

1. A
2. D
3. E
4. B
5. C

Activity 1.2 Matching Member Financial Needs to Credit Union Services

1. checking account, ATM and/or debit card
2. home purchase loan
3. life insurance
4. credit card or debit card
5. vacation club account

Activity 2.1 Comparing Account Ownerships

Type of Account Ownership	How do Sean and Rebecca own the money?	What happens to the money if Rebecca dies?
Sean and Rebecca (joint tenants WROS)	equal, 100 percent access to the account and ownership of the funds	Sean is the sole owner
Sean and Rebecca (tenants in common)	percentage ownership for each tenant	Rebecca's heirs inherit her percentage of the account
Sean and Rebecca (POD to Tara)	as joint tenants	Sean owns the money. Tara is still the beneficiary.

Member Services
ANSWERS TO ACTIVITIES

Activity 3.2 Calculating the Long-Term Effects of Compounding

1. 72 divided by 3 = 24 years
2. 116 divided by 3 = 38.7 years

Activity 3.3 Matching Member Needs to Savings Accounts

Your answers may vary but might include the following ideas.

1. A share certificate would meet their need for the highest rate of return, but they may consider depositing part of the funds in a money market if they want some of the money to be available.
2. As the money is a birthday gift, it may be an unexpected windfall. If he doesn't need the funds during the next year, he may want to consider a one-year certificate. Then, he will have money saved for a security deposit on an apartment or other moving expenses.
3. This couple sounds like their high balance would qualify them for either a certificate or a money market account. However, the money market may be best because it sounds like they want to use the money fairly soon.

Activity 5.1 Calculating Ratios

1. 25%
2. 45%

Activity 5.3 Building Your Knowledge of Loan Terminology

1. e
2. g
3. d
4. b
5. f
6. a
7. c

Appendix B Glossary

accidental death and dismemberment (AD&D) insurance Type of insurance that provides protection for the credit union and the members' surviving families against the hardship of outstanding debt in the event of one of these occurrences.

adjustable rate mortgage (ARM) Type of mortgage on which the interest rate can fluctuate.

annual percentage yield (APY) Percentage rate that reflects the total amount of dividends paid on a share account based on the dividend rate and the frequency of compounding for a 365-day period and calculated according to rules set out in the TISA.

annuity Investment offered by an insurance company and that is a fixed or variable investment that makes regular payments to the member upon maturity.

automated teller machine (ATM) Stand-alone computer terminal that allows members to directly make transactions on their accounts by using an access device such as a plastic card similar in appearance to a credit card.

automatic bill payment Automatic service under which members arrange for certain payments to be made automatically from their share draft accounts.

average daily balance method of determining account balance The credit union applies a periodic rate (such as a monthly or quarterly rate) to the average daily balance in the account for the period. The average daily balance is determined by adding the full amount of principal in the account for each day of the period and dividing the figure by the number of days in the period.

bond Long-term debt instrument that pays interest and is issued by a business, government, or government agency.

cap Interest rate limit on the amount the interest rate can change on an adjustable rate mortgage.

capacity Factor used when analyzing borrower creditworthiness; also called *ability to pay.*

character Factor used when analyzing borrower creditworthiness; also called *willingness to pay.*

closed-end credit One-time extension of credit. With closed-end credit, each loan is handled as an individual and separate transaction with a definite ending point in time.

collateral Item that secures a loan; provides something of tangible value that can be sold by the credit union in the event the member defaults on the loan.

collateralized nonpurchase money loan Type of loan that is secured with an item already owned by the member, for example, a share account loan.

contract Binding written agreement between two or more parties enforceable by law.

cosigner An individual, not necessarily a member of the credit union, who agrees to sign a legal document guaranteeing the debt of the borrowing member. If the borrower defaults, the cosigner is liable for the full amount of the loan and is obligated to pay the loan in full.

credit disability insurance Type of credit insurance that makes payments, up to the contract limit, should an insured member become disabled due to a covered accident or illness. Credit unions offer this plan to members on an optional basis.

credit life insurance Type of credit insurance under which the members' loans are reduced or paid off if they die before the loan is repaid. Credit unions offer this plan to members on an optional basis.

credit union Financial cooperative organized and controlled by individuals or groups that have a common bond. Credit union members become owners and shareholders of the credit union when they join. Members pool their assets, providing funds for loans and other financial services to those in need within the group.

credit union service organization (CUSO) For-profit corporation organized by a single credit union or group of credit unions; provides operational support to credit unions or alternative financial services to members and nonmembers.

daily balance method of determining account balance The credit union applies a daily rate to the full amount of principal in the share account each day.

debit card Card similar in appearance to an ATM card but that expands the member's ability to make transactions at other locations, such as retail stores, gas stations, and supermarket chains.

debt-to-income ratio Ratio calculated by dividing the member's total monthly income into his or her total monthly debt payments (including the payment on the loan for which he or she is applying, but not including monthly housing payment); important factor when determining capacity.

decedent Deceased person.

decedent's estate Deceased person's property.

GLOSSARY

direct deposit Automatic service under which funds are automatically transferred from another institution to the member's credit union account.

dividend Earnings on share accounts that are paid out of the earnings of a credit union and vary according to the financial performance of a credit union.

dividend rate Annual percentage that will be applied to the share account principal to calculate the dividend (not including compounding).

dormant account Inactive share account.

durable power of attorney Type of power of attorney that continues even if the member/owner is incapacitated and no longer able to make financial decisions; terminates on death of the member.

early withdrawal penalty Penalty assessed when a member withdraws funds from a share certificate before the maturity date. The calculation method is established by individual credit unions but usually involves forfeiting a sum equivalent to a certain amount of dividends.

Education IRA Type of IRA that is not actually a retirement account. It is a trust a parent or other person establishes to save money to pay for the future qualified education expenses of another person (who is under the age of eighteen while the contributions are being made). The participants have income limitations to be eligible to contribute. The amount of the annual contribution is limited and is not tax deductible. However, earnings are tax-free and withdrawals are tax-free as long as they are used to pay for the beneficiary's education expenses.

equity The difference between the home's appraised value (which is determined by a qualified appraiser) and the existing mortgage balance, if any. If the property has no mortgage, then the member's equity is the appraised value of the home.

first lien First claim to the real estate securing a mortgage should the loan go into default.

fixed rate loan Type of loan that has a rate of interest that is fixed for the term of the loan.

grace period For a credit card, the time between the date of a purchase and the date interest starts being charged on that purchase.

home equity loan Type of mortgage loan that uses residential real estate as collateral for a loan that may be a first or second mortgage; not a purchase money loan.

individual retirement account (IRA) Retirement plan that allows individuals to enjoy tax advantages and save for retirement.

interest The return paid to those who lend money to firms or others.

GLOSSARY

intestate When a person who has not made a will dies.

joint tenancy with right of survivorship (WROS) Type of account ownership that means each owner has equal, 100 percent access to the account and ownership of the funds. In the event of one owner's death, the other owners would have complete ownership of the funds.

lien Claim that a party has on the property of another party as security for payment of a debt or outstanding bill.

line of credit Pre-approved amount of credit, accessible at any time, up to the established credit limit, provided the member is not in default and remains creditworthy; payments are usually made monthly.

loan protection insurance Type of credit insurance reduces or pays off insured loan balances when members die. Total and permanent disability and joint life coverages may also be available. Provided by credit unions at no direct cost to the borrower.

MICR (Magnetic Ink Character Recognition) number Series of numbers located along the bottom of the check that contains routing and transit information, and that identifies the financial institution and the Federal Reserve Bank district in which the draft (or check) was drawn.

minor Person under the age of majority.

money market account Type of account that requires a high balance, pays high interest rates, allows deposits at any time, but has some restrictions on withdrawals, check writing, and preauthorized transfers.

mutual fund Type of investment company that makes diversified investments according to stated investment objectives and by pooling funds from a large number of investors.

open-end credit Type of credit under which the member makes a one-time application to obtain credit for use on an ongoing or revolving basis.

overdraft protection Line of credit that is combined with the member's share draft account, and doubles as overdraft protection. The member merely writes a share draft to access the line of credit.

payable on death (POD) account Type of account ownership where the account is individually or jointly owned and has a designated beneficiary. The beneficiary does not have any rights or access to the funds except in the case of the death of all the owners.

point One-time charge, sometimes called a loan origination fee, that is calculated as a percentage of the mortgage loan amount. Each point charged equals 1 percent of the principal amount of the loan.

power of attorney Document authorizing a person or persons to make withdrawals from a member's account and to conduct any other authorized transactions on behalf of the member. Can be revoked by the owner or terminates on death of the owner.

principal The amount of money on which the dividend on a savings account or interest on a loan is to be calculated.

purchase money loan Type of secured loan on which the collateral is whatever is purchased with the loan proceeds.

residual value Value of a vehicle at the end of a lease; agreed upon at the start of a lease.

right of rescission A right that means that the member has three business days to cancel the loan obligation after signing the loan documents. If the member rescinds, all charges in connection with the mortgage transaction must be refunded. Applies to home equity loans where the loan is secured by the member's principal residence and no purchase is involved.

Roth IRA Type of individual retirement account that allows individuals to make contributions that are not deductible from current income but that accumulate tax-free earnings. Distributions are therefore tax-free. These plans have income limits for determining who is eligible to contribute and how much can be contributed. At age 59 ½, the account owner can withdraw funds without taxes or penalties as long as the account has been open for at least five tax years.

Rule of 72 Method for roughly calculating the number of years it will take savings to double in value; divide 72 by the annual percentage rate.

Rule of 116 Method for roughly calculating the number of years it will take savings to triple in value; divide 116 by the annual percentage rate.

second mortgage Loan made on real estate that already has a first mortgage. A first mortgage has priority over a second mortgage in case of loan default and foreclosure.

secured loan A loan that has collateral. Collateral on a loan provides something of value that can be sold or kept by the credit union in the event the member defaults on the loan.

share Set amount of money a member deposits in a credit union to become a member.

share account loan Type of loan secured by all or a portion of a savings account at the credit union.

share certificate Type of savings account that requires the member to keep their funds in the account for a specified period of time, called the term of the account. If the member wants to withdraw funds before the maturity date, the credit union usually assesses a penalty.

share draft Document similar to a check that is a written order to a financial institution from the member/customer to pay a specified amount of money to another party upon demand.

signature loan Type of loan that is made solely on the strength of the member's personal creditworthiness; also called an unsecured loan.

Simplified Employee Pension (SEP) Plan Type of individual retirement account plan an employer uses to make contributions to employees' retirement accounts. Each participant owns an IRA that receives the contributions under the SEP program. The employer's retirement contributions are divided among the participants according to a formula. The employer decides each year how much (if any) to contribute to the SEP program for that year.

stock Share of direct ownership interest in a company.

stop payment order System whereby a member authorizes the credit union to refuse payment on a share draft the member has written to another party.

tenancy in common Type of account ownership that gives the multiple owners ownership of and access to only a portion of the account funds. The percentage of ownership for each tenant depends on the terms of the account. Tenancy in common does not have a right of survivorship. On the death of one of the owners of the tenancy in common, the deceased person's interest in the account passes to his or her estate. It does not pass to the other account tenants.

term life insurance Life insurance plan that provides protection for a set period of time, such as five, ten, or twenty years.

testate When a person dies after making a will.

tiered rate A type of interest rate on some money market accounts. The account earns one rate on a specified balance and a higher rate if the balance exceeds a set amount.

total obligations-to-income ratio Type of ratio that includes the member's housing payment in the total monthly debt payments; factor when determining borrower's capacity.

traditional IRA Type of individual retirement account that allows members to contribute part or all of their compensation (for example wages and salary) to an account. The amount contributed is limited by law and may be deductible or nondeductible from federal income taxes for the year it is contributed. The amount of an individual's income limits the contributed amount that can be deferred from current income taxes. While the contributions remain in the account, the earnings are tax-deferred until they are taken out of the account.

truncation Check or share draft storage system whereby cancelled share drafts are not returned to the member with the monthly statement.

Uniform Gifts/Transfers to Minors Act State law that provides for a type of account ownership under which an adult controls the funds in the account but a minor owns the account. When the child reaches the age of majority, the funds must be turned over to him or her.

unsecured loan Type of loan that is made solely on the strength of the member's personal creditworthiness; also called a *signature loan*.

variable-rate loan Type of loan on which the interest rate fluctuates, depending on current market rates.

voice response unit (VRU) Type of technology that allows members to access accounts by pressing buttons on the phone keypad.

whole life insurance Type of life insurance intended to provide coverage over the member's whole life rather than a set term.

will Legal document that specifies how to dispose of a decedent's property (or estate) after death.

Appendix C Resources

Learning Opportunities from the Center for Professional Development

The CUNA Center for Professional Development (CPD) designs training materials specific to credit unions. CPD resources are available to help develop credit union careers in all areas of operations. Participants can also take many CPD certificate courses for college credit by studying alone, in informal groups, or as part of a formal credit union training program.

For more information about CPD training, you may

- browse the categories of training resources listed here for options that fit your needs, then
- call your state league education director, or
- call CUNA customer service at (800)356-8010, extension 4157, or
- explore CUNA's web site at *www.cuna.org*.

Certificate Programs

STAR (Staff Training and Recognition Program)

The Staff Training and Recognition (STAR) program provides self-study courses on a wide range of topics. STAR training strengthens your staff's skills, builds a solid base of credit union knowledge, and adds power to your products and services. Everyone wins with STAR.

To order STAR modules, contact your state league representative.

Relevant STAR modules include:

S100-JK1 Money and Negotiable Instruments

Learn how to prevent fraud with proven methods for detecting counterfeit money and recognizing bad checks. Improve efficiency and accuracy by understanding the methods for handling cash; and accepting deposits, share drafts, and traveler's checks.

S120-JK1 Cross-Selling

This course helps staff realize that selling is positive. They'll discover the fundamentals of cross-selling, marketing, sales presentations, and telemarketing. These skills encourage success through personal and professional interaction.

S500-JK1 Improving and Maintaining Quality Service

Discover the importance of developing a sales culture—no longer a luxury for credit unions. Provide front-line staff with practical advice for developing quality service, overcoming barriers, and maintaining a positive sales attitude.

S510-JK1 Successful Sales Techniques

Gain practical advice, sales tools, and proven techniques to succeed in sales. Understand how to maintain a sales culture, how to listen, the importance of product knowledge, and the power of words in selling.

S520-JK1 Interpersonal Skills: Understanding Your Impact on Members

Discover the tools needed to enhance critical interpersonal skills, and understand the impact of communication and interpersonal style. Employees will learn and understand the importance of positive interaction with problem members.

S1100-JK1 Working Effectively with Difficult Members and Staff

This course helps employees understand why incidents of anger, conflict, or even violence occur in the workplace. Employees gain the tools they require to understand personalities and deal with difficult people. They will develop listening, communicating, and negotiating skills; and learn how to anticipate difficult situations.

S1110-JK1 Helping Members Understand and Solve Problems: Your Role as Financial Educator

Discover the importance that front-line staff has as member educators. This course teaches employees to focus on helping members understand your credit union's financial products and services. Employees will learn why member education is important, what it takes to become an educator, how to recognize learning opportunities, and how to build member relationships.

S1120-JK1 Using Technology to Improve Member Service

This course helps employees understand the changing role of front-line staff, communicate with members about technology, understand critical technologies, and cross-sell remote services. Employees learn through informative case studies. This module adds additional insight into the critical role of technology for those employees who have completed the Technology track.

MERIT (Management Training Recognition Program)

This program helps credit union employees develop the skills needed for management success. It includes modules on leadership, communication, employee relations, conflict management, team building, marketing, and strategic management. Completion of MERIT courses creates opportunities to move up the career ladder and shows upper management a commitment to a credit union career.

To order MERIT modules, contact your state league representative. Relevant MERIT modules include:

M15-JK1 Interpersonal Skills: Understanding Your Effect on Others

Your leadership role means you're in the people business. This course helps you to understand your interpersonal style and its effect on others, read nonverbal cues, know when to be flexible, and communicate effectively.

M16-JK1 Leading and Managing Credit Union Sales

This is a comprehensive guide to develop and manage a sales and service force. Learn how to develop a sales planning system, write strategies, organize an effective sales operation, develop a sales culture, communicate with members, and evaluate your sales operation.

M17-JK1 Credit Union Financial Management for Nonfinancial Executives

This module presents an efficient overview of credit union financial operations. This easy-to-understand course includes information on capital adequacy, asset-liability management, cash flow forecasting, spread analysis, and ratio analysis. Learn about balance sheets, income statements, and risk management.

M30-JK1 Managing Financial Education Programs

At a time when bankruptcies are at historic highs and more members than ever need help in managing their money, the credit union has a golden opportunity to build relationships through financial education programs. The course shows how to help members create a secure financial future for themselves and their families.

Handbooks

CUNA's Center for Professional Development publishes noncertificate books (handbooks) that serve as references and resources for specific areas and topics. Visit the CUNA web site or phone customer service for details and assistance in choosing the resources that best fit your needs.

Member Services
RESOURCES

Any of the handbooks listed here can be ordered with the order form in the back of this book or by calling CUNA Customer Service at (800)356-8010, ext. 4157.

Business Development Series: Electronic Services

This book, one in a series of three on business development, examines how credit unions can use technology more effectively and profitably. The goal is to improve the bottom line and, at the same time, achieve the highest possible level of member satisfaction. The handbook also examines questions such as:

- How can technology help credit unions cement bonds with members?
- What business reasons are there for adopting technology?
- Which members are likely to be attracted by various technologies?
- What types of support—in terms of training, marketing, or technical help—are needed or desirable?
- What advantages and disadvantages does the technology carry?
- What can be learned from those who have gone first?

Business Development Series: Electronic Services promotes a sensible approach to technology—based on the premise that technology for its own sake is a waste of money.
#22894-JK1, 129 pages, $29.95, 2000

Checks & Share Drafts: Teller & Member Service Handbook

A teller's job can be stressful, especially when faced with check-cashing situations that require prompt action. But many tellers are trained in only the basics of checks and share drafts before being placed on the teller line. They may not recognize potentially fraudulent checks, or may not be confident in dealing with those that are unusual or require special processing. This book

- defines the differences between share drafts, checks, and other negotiable instruments;
- helps tellers understand requirements for cashing and depositing drafts and checks:
- covers a range of topics from endorsements to multi-party checks;
- alerts tellers to problems or concerns with certain drafts and checks.

Checks & Share Drafts is a handy reference for tellers and member service representatives to use at their work stations or elsewhere!
#22643-JK1, 142 pages, $29.95, 2000

Communication Skills: Teller & Member Service Handbook

The *Communications Skills* handbook helps tellers and member service representatives communicate effectively with people of differing backgrounds, ages and personalities. This handbook

- offers real-life examples;
- helps tellers deal with those who may be irate or abusive, bossy or critical, upset or confused;
- gives guidance on communicating with senior citizens or persons who may have special needs;
- gives tips on how to remain poised in any given situation.

Communication Skills helps staff learn how to create a positive working environment and become part of the credit union team. This handbook is designed for member services staff, but useful to *everyone* who wants to become a more effective communicator!
#22644-JK1, 139 pages, $29.95, 2000

Credit Union Accounts: Teller & Member Service Handbook

Tellers and member-contact staff need to understand the various accounts offered by the credit union. This book starts them off with important definitions, features, and benefits of the various accounts. A deeper understanding of credit union accounts allows tellers to explain these accounts to members, and provide better service. *Credit Union Accounts* covers

- the basics of IRAs, money market accounts, CDs, and account-related aspects of bonds and loans;
- the history behind the various accounts;
- regulatory concerns.

This information helps tellers and member service representatives serve members with confidence, and use their knowledge of account services to expand their careers within the credit union.
#22642-JK1, 116 pages, $29.95, 2000

Credit Union Teller Handbook, 3rd Edition

For many members, tellers personify the credit union. This handbook introduces new tellers to

- the "people helping people" philosophy of credit unions;
- the diverse products and services credit unions offer;
- the people and technical skills they must possess and continue to develop;
- cash and check handling procedures to ensure accuracy and efficient service;

- fraud prevention;
- special and emergency situations.

New to this third edition are sections on translating financial jargon to terms members will understand, instructions on identifying and correcting common mistakes, and the most current procedures to head off fraud. The third edition expands emphasis on the teller's role in marketing credit union products and services and acknowledges the wider array of electronic services. Also new is a glossary defining key terms.
#22823-JK1, 125 pages, $24.95, 2000

Essentials for New Credit Union Employees Kit

This creative "kit in a box" provides coordinated tools to develop guided instruction to new employees. It presents and reinforces the history, philosophy and structure of the credit union system, as well as day-to-day operational and member-service skills. Each component reinforces the others, making the most of training sessions. The kit includes

- a comprehensive leader's guide with lesson plans;
- a diskette for convenience in developing custom lesson plans;
- five fun and fast-moving participant's guides;
- four insightful videotapes;
- a set of overhead masters.

The kit also includes popular games to increase comprehension and strengthen interpersonal skills.
#21348-JK1, $499.00, 1995

People, Not Profit; The Story of the Credit Union Movement, 3rd edition

People, Not Profit is one of the most popular versions of the credit union story. This edition highlights every significant point in American credit union development—from the early years of struggle, through the remarkable growth and development of the last five decades, including how credit unions mobilized to pass H.R. 1151 and preserve the credit union alternative for consumers. It chronicles the persistent challenges from the banking industry—each of them ultimately resulting in grassroots victories for credit unions. This compact revised manual helps to

- instill commitment in employees and volunteers through orientation and training;
- market our unique cooperative advantage;
- improve member awareness of the credit union;

- serve as the basis of community activities and information campaigns.

People, Not Profit prepares people at all levels for the challenges we now face, and helps convey to members the qualities that can be found only in credit unions.

#22228-JK1, 96 pages, $24.95, 1999

The Power of Business Ethics: Credit Union Ideals in the Real World

The Power of Business Ethics takes on the 150-year history of cooperative credit and shows how our values are prized in today's economic environment. Credit Unions have a huge advantage in marketing our cooperative difference. *The Power of Business Ethics* provokes readers to understand our fascinating, unique story and build on it for even greater success. This book includes

- a unique perspective that shows why credit unions are a special breed;
- ethical standards for employers;
- ethical standards for employees;
- ethics and the member;
- ethics and the community;
- communicating ethical standards.

#23166-JK1, $29.95, March, 2001

Real Stories from Credit Unions

Now the credit union movement has a collection of from-the-heart stories of mission in action! With humor and drama, these true stories share the optimism, caring, and can-do triumphs of ordinary people who make extraordinary dreams come true. These vibrant stories

- personalize mission;
- demonstrate the high-risk/high-reward equation;
- inspire the efforts of all those "making the difference;"
- validate the strategic aims of Project Differentiation.

In the deepest sense, this book has as many "authors" as there are stories. From eight-year-old Gianni, saving for college at his credit union since age two; to Walter, a high school grad with his heart set on buying a home for his grandparents; to Ann Mary Bukenya who borrowed from the midwives' credit union to finance her Kyengera Maternity Home in Uganda—people throughout the movement unfold the story of credit union empowerment.

#23327-JK1, 104 pages, $39.95, 2001

Member Services

RESOURCES

Youth Financial Literacy: Preparing Youth for Financial Responsibility

This handbook offers suggestions for developing formal financial curricula in schools; building community awareness of the need for financial education; and getting parents, educators, administrators, and students involved in the process. Included are ways to educate young members on the value of saving, strategies for managing personal finances, and healthy credit practices. *Youth Financial Literacy* also covers

- developing highly focused relationships with youth
- strengthening relationships with parents
- providing training seminars for youth and parents
- building rapport with school systems
- becoming involved in community programs for youth
- preparing Internet pages to educate youth
- developing a youth program as part of the credit union's overall objectives and goals

The handbook provides case studies of specific credit unions' youth programs, classroom presentation, community activities, seminars, and special promotions.

#22646-JK1, 141 pages, $29.95, 1999

Web Sites

http://www.cuna.com The official site of Credit Union National Association

http://www.ncua.gov The official site of the National Credit Union Administration

Appendix D Test Questions

Answers to these test questions are to be marked on either the scannable answer sheet or competency test provided. Please do not mark answers in the module or return these pages to be graded. Photocopies of scannable answer sheets and competency tests will not be accepted. Original scannable answer sheets are to be returned to CUNA in the envelope provided. Original competency tests are to be returned to your league education department.

1. Which of the following is a reason to learn basic information about the full range of your credit union's services?
    a. prepare for a career move into management
    b. make cross-sales
    c. give tax and legal advice to members
    d. all of the above

2. What type of financial need is most likely when a member says, "We want to buy a house this year"?
    a. need for emergency cash
    b. need to make payments and handle daily cash flow
    c. need to borrow money to achieve a long-term goal
    d. need to control risk of disastrous and sudden losses

3. What is the most important source of funds for credit union loans?
    a. money credit unions borrow from banks
    b. money credit unions raise by selling stock
    c. money members deposit in savings and transaction accounts
    d. money members donate to the credit union

4. What is a for-profit corporation organized by a credit union or group of credit unions to provide services to credit unions, members, and nonmembers?
    a. financial services institution
    b. credit union service organization
    c. credit union agency
    d. support services corporation

Member Services
TEST QUESTIONS

5. If Braden and Susan own an account in joint tenancy, what happens to the money if Braden dies?
   a. Braden's heirs inherit his share of the account.
   b. The beneficiary on the account becomes a joint tenant.
   c. A new joint tenant must be appointed by Susan.
   d. Susan owns the money in the account.

6. With a payable on death account, who can make a withdrawal during the life of the owner?
   a. only the account beneficiary
   b. only the owner of the account
   c. either the beneficiary or the owner
   d. the beneficiary and the owner must both sign for a withdrawal

7. The phrase that best describes the term "power of attorney" is the ability of
   a. a specific person to act legally on behalf of another individual.
   b. members to bring class action suits.
   c. a legal fraternity to prosecute managers.
   d. any attorney to access a member's account.

8. Why must credit unions obtain a tax identification number on all savings accounts?
   a. to qualify borrowers for risk-based lending
   b. so that the credit union can obtain a credit report
   c. to verify accountholder identity and to avoid being penalized by the federal government
   d. to meet requirements of the NCUA

9. What information is typically included in an account agreement?
   a. rules for honoring checks or drafts
   b. any restrictions on withdrawals
   c. how the credit union determines who can withdraw
   d. all of the above

10. What is the function of a state probate court?
    a. determines when inactive accounts must be turned over to the state government
    b. has jurisdiction over lawsuits brought against credit unions
    c. administers property for incompetent persons
    d. oversees the proper distribution of a decedent's estate

11. The amount of money in an account on which a dividend is calculated is called the
    a. principal.
    b. loan balance.
    c. earnings.
    d. interest.

12. The percentage rate that reflects the total amount of dividends paid and the effects of compounding is the
    a. annual percentage rate.
    b. nominal rate.
    c. annual percentage yield.
    d. dividend rate.

13. Applying the compounding Rule of 72, how long would it take for a member's account balance to double at 3% interest?
    a. 12 years
    b. 16 years
    c. 20 years
    d. 24 years

14. What is the purpose of share insurance?
    a. pays out a death benefit to the policy beneficiary if a member dies
    b. makes a member's loan payments in case of total disability
    c. ensures that members savings are protected if a credit union fails and is closed
    d. provides a monthly payment after a member retires

15. When do credit unions typically allow the funds in a two-year share certificate to be withdrawn without penalty?
    a. after the account has been opened for one month
    b. after the end of the first year of the term
    c. within two weeks before the maturity date
    d. on the maturity date

16. MICR numbers on share drafts help computers do which of the following?
    a. identify, route, sort, forward, and pay the draft
    b. clearly identify the payee, the payer, and the amount
    c. calculate interest rates and track marketing efforts
    d. send notice to members who need to reorder share drafts

17. "Truncating share drafts" is most accurately described as
    a. a method of processing share drafts in which canceled drafts are not returned to members.
    b. duplicating share drafts electronically.
    c. being able to offer share drafts at a discount without service charges.
    d. providing share drafts that are smaller in size than standard checks.

Member Services
TEST QUESTIONS

18. When a member authorizes the credit union to refuse payment on a share draft the member has written to another person, this is called a
    a. stop payment.
    b. nonsufficient funds draft.
    c. payment refusal.
    d. dormant draft.

19. Which statement correctly describes overdraft protection on share draft accounts?
    a. Protects against fraudulent drafts from being accepted.
    b. Requires payroll checks to be directly deposited into a share draft account.
    c. Provides access to preapproved credit and prevents a draft from being returned for nonsufficient funds.
    d. Automatically stops payment on an overdrawn share draft account.

20. Surveys have shown that _____ are foundation services for developing a strong relationship with members.
    a. savings accounts
    b. ATM cards
    c. share draft accounts
    d. personal loans

21. A closed-end loan is
    a. the last loan a member is allowed to take.
    b. a loan that can be issued through the use of a credit card.
    c. always due thirty-six months from the date of the loan.
    d. a onetime extension of credit.

22. Which of the following is a characteristic of closed-end credit?
    a. typically used for home equity lines of credit
    b. number of payments and maturity date are calculated precisely
    c. requires supervisory committee approval
    d. may be used on an ongoing or revolving basis

23. Which of the following is a characteristic of open-end credit?
    a. number of payments and maturity date is calculated precisely
    b. may be used on an ongoing or revolving basis
    c. requires supervisory committee approval
    d. typically used for mortgage loans

24. According to the text, creditworthiness is based on what three factors?
    a. character, capacity, collateral
    b. collateral, cash, savings
    c. home equity, credit history, cash
    d. liquidity, delinquency, capacity

Member Services
TEST QUESTIONS

25. If a member has $2,000 per month in income and has $400 per month in consumer debt, the member's debt-to-income ratio is
    a. 20 percent.
    b. 17 percent.
    c. 12 percent.
    d. 10 percent.

26. Why are signature loans riskier for credit unions than many other types of loans?
    a. Interest rates for signature loans are usually low.
    b. Terms and interest rates for signature loans are fixed.
    c. Borrowers are entitled to a right of rescission.
    d. The loan is granted without collateral being required.

27. What is the most effective strategy for the credit union to increase loan volume?
    a. Borrow more money to make more loans.
    b. Call back funds invested in the stock portfolio.
    c. Lower loan rates.
    d. Review the debt-to-income ratio in the loan department.

28. Interest rates on variable rate loans move up or down depending on which of the following?
    a. the earnings of the credit union
    b. Truth-in-Lending regulations
    c. member's debt-to-income ratio
    d. current market rates

29. A grace period is
    a. a probationary period for new employees.
    b. the time between the date of a credit card purchase and the date interest begins to be charged to that purchase.
    c. the point at which payments to principal become larger than payments to interest on a mortgage loan.
    d. the point at which a salary increase appears on the employee's next paycheck.

30. Which of the following type of loan is secured by the item purchased with the loan proceeds?
    a. signature loan
    b. collateralized nonpurchase money loan
    c. purchase money loan
    d. share secured loan

31. If a member finances a $100,000 mortgage and is charged two points, what is the total dollar amount paid for the points?
    a. $20,000
    b. $10,000
    c. $2,500
    d. $2,000

Member Services
TEST QUESTIONS

32. What is home equity?
    a. the difference between a home's appraised value and the mortgage balance
    b. the current balance of the mortgage loan
    c. a home's sale price
    d. a valuation of property by an appraiser

33. When funds are automatically transferred from another institution to the member's share draft account, the service is called
    a. automatic payment.
    b. electronic benefit payment.
    c. telephone transfer.
    d. direct deposit.

34. The technology that allows members to access accounts by making a telephone call and pressing buttons on the telephone keypad is called
    a. an ATM.
    b. a voice response unit.
    c. Internet financial services.
    d. a debit card.

35. What must an ATM owner do if it charges fees for using the machine?
    a. allow users to cancel transactions before being charged
    b. charge no more than $2.00 per transaction
    c. provide one free transaction before charging the fee
    d. all of the above

36. Why are some members concerned about using Internet financial services?
    a. They worry about the security of transmitted information.
    b. Errors cannot be traced and corrected.
    c. Incompatibility of different computer systems with the Internet.
    d. All of the above.

37. The dollar amount of a postal money order cannot exceed
    a. $500.
    b. $700.
    c. $1,000.
    d. $1,500.

38. It's a good idea to store _____ in a safe deposit box.
    a. a will
    b. a birth certificate
    c. burial instructions
    d. a large amount of cash

39. A type of life insurance that provides protection for a set number of years and has no cash value is
    a. whole life insurance.
    b. universal life insurance.
    c. term life insurance.
    d. an annuity.

40. An investment company that makes diversified investments by pooling funds from a large number of investors is a/an
    a. stock.
    b. mutual fund.
    c. bond.
    d. annuity.

Member Services
TEST QUESTIONS

Evaluation Questions

Please complete these evaluation questions after you have taken the test. Mark appropriate answers on the scannable answer sheet or competency test under numbers 41 through 44.

41. I am taking this module through
    a. correspondence.
    b. chapter/credit union study group.
    c. league-sponsored conference or workshop.
    d. credit union in-house training program.

42. Overall, I feel this module was
    a. excellent.
    b. good.
    c. fair.
    d. poor.

43. This module was
    a. practical.
    b. interesting.
    c. irrelevant.
    d. boring.

44. The competency test was
    a. fair.
    b. clear.
    c. tricky.
    d. vague.

Index

(Page numbers shown in italic type refer to figures, tables or similar material.)

A

accidental death and dismemberment insurance, 131–32
account access, Internet-based, 111, *117–21*
account agreements, 18, 23, *24–26,* 56
account balances, calculating, 36–37
account disclosures, 27
accounts, membership. *See* membership accounts
account statements
    savings accounts, 41
    share draft accounts, 56, *57–58*
accrued dividends, 37
adjustable rate mortgages (ARMs), 94
advertising, Internet-based, 108–9
agricultural loans, 101
annual percentage yield, 37–38, *39*
annuities, 134
application forms
    credit insurance, 78
    loans, *70, 113–17*
    membership accounts, 18, *19–23*
appraisal fees, 94–95
appraisals, 92
auto loans and leases, 73, 89–91
automated teller machines (ATMs), 105–7
automatic bill payment, 104
average daily balance method, 37

B

balances, calculating, 36–37
balancing services, 63
balloon payments, 68
beneficiaries
    for life savings insurance, 44–45
    for membership accounts, 29
    for POD accounts, 15

bill payment
    automatic, 104
    online, 111, *122–23*
bonds, 133–34
brochures, 4
brokerage services, 10, 133–34
business accounts, 16
business loans, 88–89, 101

C

capacity to repay, 71
caps on ARMs, 94
certificates of deposit. *See* share certificates
character, 69
checking accounts. *See* share draft accounts
children's clubs, 30, *31*
children's Web pages, 109
Christmas club accounts, 29
clearing process, 53–54, 136–37
closed accounts, 28
closed-end credit, 68
closing fees, 94–95
collateral, 71, 72, 100–101. *See also* secured loans
collateralized non-purchase money loans, 89
competition, 5, 76
compounding dividends, 37–38, *39, 40*
consumer literature, 32
contracts, 18
cosigners, 81–82
counseling (retirement), 32
credit card accounts, 82–87
credit disability insurance, 77–79
credit insurance, 76–79
credit life insurance, 77
credit reports, 69–71, 95

INDEX

credit scores, 71
credit union account transfers, 104
credit unions defined, 13
credit union service organizations (CUSOs), 9–11
creditworthiness, 69–71, 94
cross-sales, 5
custodial accounts, 15

D

daily balance method, 36–37
dealer financing arrangements, 90
debit cards, 107, *108*
debt-to-income ratio, 71
decedent accounts, 28–29
direct deposit, 60, 104
disability insurance, 77–79
disclosures, 27
discount directories, 32
dividends, 35–39, *40,* 53
documentation
    account agreements, 18, 23, *24–26*
    account disclosures, 27
    account statements, 41, 56, *57–58*
    identification cards, 27
    insurance applications, *78*
    loan applications, *70*
    membership application forms, 18, *19–23*
    rate sheets, *39, 42–43*
    signature cards, 26
dormant accounts, 28
durable power of attorney, 17–18

E

early distributions, 48–50
early withdrawal penalties, 46
education IRAs, 50–51
education loans, 87–88
equity, 95–96
estates, 29
events, as special services, 32
extensions on loans, 68–69

F

farm loans, 101
fast approval, 90
fees
    ATM, 106
    credit card accounts, 87
    mortgage loans, 94–95
    reduced, 32
    savings accounts, 40–41, *42–43*
    share draft accounts, 62–64
FFEL loans, 87–88
filing fees, 95
finance charges, 84
financial education, 130
financial planning services, 10, 132–33
first liens, 92
first mortgage loans, 92–95
fixed loan rates, 76
future services, 5–6, 134–37

G

grace periods, 84

H

home equity lines of credit, 97–98
home equity loans, 95–97
home mortgage loans, 92–95

I

identification cards, 27
inactive accounts, 28
income tax preparation, 10
individual retirement accounts (IRAs), 48–51
information, online, 108–9
insurance
    credit insurance, 76–79
    from CUSOs, 11, 131–32
    life savings, 44–45
    miscellaneous services, 130–32
    share insurance, 41, 44

interactive features, online, 109
interest rates, 72–76, 94
Internet-based transactions, 107–24
intestate, 29
investment services, 10, 133–34

J

joint tenancy, 14, 29

L

"lease look-alike" loans, 91
leasing, 90–91
liens, 90, 92
life insurance, 132
life savings insurance, 44–45
lines of credit
    home equity, 97–98
    personal, 63–64, 82
loan protection insurance, 77
loans
    categorizing, 67
    credit insurance, 76–79
    creditworthiness, 69–71, 94
    interest rates, 72–76, 94
    open- versus closed-end, 68
    overview, 8
    payment schedules, 68–69
    real estate, 10–11, 92–95
    secured loan types, 89–101
    secured versus unsecured, 71–72
    unsecured loan types, 81–89

M

meetings and events, 32
member identification cards, 27
member service
    meeting needs, 6, 64–66
    quality, 4–5
membership accounts
    closed and dormant, 28
    decedent, 28–29
    documentation, 18–27
    key concepts, 13
    ownership types, 14–18
    special services, 29–33

membership application forms, 18, *19–23*
MEMBERS Prime Club, 32
member surveys, 109
MICR numbers, 55, *56*
minimum balance requirements, 40, 60
money market accounts, 46–48
money orders, 127–28
monthly service charges, 62
monthly statements
    savings accounts, 41
    share draft accounts, 56, *57–58*
mortgage loans, 92–95
mutual funds, 134

N

National Credit Union Administration (NCUA), 44
National Credit Union Share Insurance Fund, 44
needs, 6
nongrace cards, 84
nonsufficient funds, 62–63
notary services, 129

O

older members, services for, 30–33
online transactions, 107–24
open-end credit, 68
operational support, from CUSOs, 9
organization accounts, 16
overdraft protection, 63–64, 82

P

payable on death accounts, 15, *16*
payment schedules, 68–69
payroll deposit, 60, 104
personal property, as collateral, 100
personal service, 124–25
PLUS loans, 87–88
POD accounts, 15, *16*
points, 94
power of attorney, 16–18
preapproval, 90

prepayments, 69
prestige cards, 87
primary financial institution status, 64
principal, 36
printing fees, 62
professional referrals, 4
purchase money loans, 89

R

real estate lending, 10–11, 92–95
referrals, 4
repayment patterns, 71
repayment risk, 73
repayment terms (credit card), 84
residual value, 90
retirement accounts, 48–51
retirement counseling, 32
revolving credit, 83
right of recission, 96–97
risk management, 6, 73
Roth IRAs, 50
Rule of 72, 38
Rule of 116, 38

S

safe deposit boxes, 128–29
savings accounts
    dividends, 35–39, *40*
    fees and requirements, 40–41, *42–43*
    insurance, 41–45
    types, 7–8, 45–51
savings clubs, 29–30, *31*
savings goal accounts, 29–30
second mortgages, 95
secured loans
    basic features, 72, 89
    first mortgage loans, 92–95
    home equity, 95–97
    home equity lines of credit, 97–98
    other collateral, 100–101
    vehicle loans and leases, 73, 89–91
secured personal loans, 89
securities
    brokerage services, 10, 133–34
    as collateral, 100

security, 111, 136
senior citizen services, 30–33
services overview, 3–9
share accounts, 13, 45. *See also* savings accounts
share certificates, 45–46, *47*
share draft accounts
    basic features, 56–59
    benefits to credit unions, 64–66
    fees and services, 62–64, 82
    overview, 53–55
    types, 60, *61*
share insurance, 41, 44
share-secured loans, 73, 100
signature cards, 26
signature loans, 72, 81–82
simplified employee pension plans, 50
smart cards, 134
sole account ownership, 14
special member group accounts, 29–33, 60
Stafford loans, 87
statements
    savings accounts, 41
    share draft accounts, 56, *57–58*
stocks, 100, 133
stop payment orders, 62, *63*
stored value cards, 134
support services, 9
survivorship rights, 14, 15

T

tax benefits, 48, 97
telephone services, 104–5
tenancy in common, 15
term life insurance, 132
testate, 29
tiered rates, 46–48
time, in dividend calculations, 36
title examination fees, 95
total obligations-to-income, 71
traditional IRAs, 48–50
transaction account types, 7–8. *See also* savings accounts; share draft accounts
transaction limits (money market), 46

INDEX

transaction rules (savings accounts), 41
transaction systems
    ATM and debit cards, 105–7
    automatic transfers, 104
    Internet-based, 107–24
    overview, 8–9, 103
    personal service and, 124–25
    telephone services, 104–5
travel agency services, 11
traveler's checks, 128, *130*
truncation, 56–59

U

underwriting, 69–71, 94
Uniform Gifts/Transfers to Minors Act, 15
unsecured loans
    basic features, 72
    business loans, 88–89
    credit card accounts, 82–87
    education loans, 87–88
    lines of credit, 63–64, 82
    signature loans, 72, 81–82

V

variable loan rates, 76
vehicle loans and leases, 73, 89–91
voice response units, 104–5
volume, loan rates and, 76

W

web-based transactions, 107–24
whole life insurance, 132
wills, 29, 129

Y

youth clubs, 30

CUNA & Affiliates Order Form

Call To place an order or ask a question:
(800)356-8010, press 3
(or dial ext. 4157)
7:30 a.m. to 6:00 p.m.
Monday–Friday, CST
Local calls (608)231-4157
TTY phone (800)356-8030

Fax (608)231-1869

Mail the order form to:
CUNA Customer Service
P.O. Box 333
Madison, WI 53701–0333

E-mail customerservice@cuna.com

Ship to:

Credit union

Attention

Street address for shipping

City/State/Zip

Bill to:

Credit union

Attention   Title

Address

City/State/Zip

Phone   Ext. #

Fax

Payment method
☐ Credit unions in U.S.:
No need to prepay, we'll bill you for the total amount of your order.

☐ Individuals and International customers:
Must prepay in U.S. dollars.

Quantity	Stock Number	Description	Unit Price	Total

Subtotal: We'll calculate the freight and handling (plus sales tax if applicable).

Prices subject to change based on reprints and revisions.

Thank you for your order!